S0-BMU-407

180 Days of LANGUAGE for Third Grade

The excited bird

- ✓ capitalization
- ✓ punctuation
- ✓ parts of speech
- ✓ spelling

Author
Christine Dugan, M.A.Ed.

SHELL EDUCATION

Image Credits

All images Shutterstock

Standards

© Copyright 2010. National Governors Association Center for Best Practices and Council of Chief State School Officers. All rights reserved.

Shell Education

5301 Oceanus Drive
Huntington Beach, CA 92649-1030
http://www.shelleducation.com

ISBN 978-1-4258-1168-6

© 2015 Shell Education Publishing, Inc.

TABLE OF CONTENTS

INTRODUCTION AND RESEARCH

People who love the English language often lament the loss of grammar knowledge and the disappearance of systematic grammar instruction. We wince at emails with errors, such as when the noun *advice* is used instead of the verb *advise*. We may set aside a résumé with the incorrect placement of an apostrophe. And some of us pore (not pour) over entertaining punctuation guides such as *Eats, Shoots and Leaves* by Lynne Truss (2003). We chuckle over collections of bloopers such as *Anguished English: An Anthology of Accidental Assaults upon Our Language* by Richard Lederer (1987).

Even though we worry about grammar, our students arrive at school with a complex set of grammar rules in place—albeit affected by the prevailing dialect (Hillocks and Smith 2003, 727). For example, while students may not be able to recite the rule for where to position an adjective, they know intuitively to say *the yellow flower* instead of *the flower yellow*. All this knowledge comes without formal instruction. Further, young people easily shift between articulating or writing traditional patterns of grammar and communicating complete sentences with startling efficiency: IDK (I don't know), and for the ultimate in brevity, K (okay).

So, if students speak fairly well and have already mastered a complex written shorthand, why study grammar? Researchers provide us with three sound reasons:

1. the insights it offers into the way the language works

2. its usefulness in mastering standard forms of English

3. its usefulness in improving composition skills (Hillocks and Smith 1991, 594)

INTRODUCTION AND RESEARCH *(cont.)*

Studying grammar also provides users—teachers, students, and parents—with a common vocabulary to discuss both spoken and written language. The Assembly for the Teaching of English Grammar states, "Grammar is important because it is the language that makes it possible for us to talk about language. Grammar names the types of words and word groups that make up sentences not only in English but in any language. As human beings, we can put sentences together even as children—we all *do* grammar. But to be able to talk about how sentences are built, about the types of words and word groups that make up sentences—that is *knowing about* grammar."

With the publication of the Common Core State Standards, key instructional skills are identified, such as identifying parts of speech, using prepositional phrases, capitalizing, and correctly using commas. Writing conventions such as punctuation serve an important function for the reader—setting off syntactic units and providing intonational cues and semantic information. Capitalization provides the reader with such cues as sentence beginnings and proper nouns (Hodges, 1991, 779).

The Need for Practice

To be successful in today's classroom, students must deeply understand both concepts and procedures so that they can discuss and demonstrate their understanding. Demonstrating understanding is a process that must be continually practiced in order for students to be successful. According to Marzano, "practice has always been, and always will be, a necessary ingredient to learning procedural knowledge at a level at which students execute it independently" (2010, 83). Practice is especially important to help students apply their concrete, conceptual understanding of a particular language skill.

Understanding Assessment

In addition to providing opportunities for frequent practice, teachers must be able to assess students' comprehension and word-study skills. This is important so that teachers can adequately address students' misconceptions, build on their current understanding, and challenge them appropriately. Assessment is a long-term process that often involves careful analysis of student responses from a lesson discussion, project, practice sheet, or test. When analyzing the data, it is important for teachers to reflect on how their teaching practices may have influenced students' responses, and to identify those areas where additional instruction may be required. In short, the data gathered from assessments should be used to inform instruction: slow down, speed up, or reteach. This type of assessment is called *formative assessment*.

HOW TO USE THIS BOOK

With *180 Days of Language,* students receive practice with punctuation, identifying parts of speech, capitalization, and spelling. The daily practice will develop students' writing efforts and oral reading skills.

Easy to Use and Standards-Based

These activities reinforce grade-level skills across a variety of language concepts. The questions are provided as a full practice page, making them easy to prepare and implement as part of a classroom morning routine, at the beginning of each language arts lesson, or as homework.

Every practice page provides questions that are tied to a language standard. Students are given opportunities for regular practice in language skills, allowing them to build confidence through these quick standards-based activities.

Question	Language Skill	Common Core State Standard
1–2	punctuation or capitalization	**Language Anchor Standard 3.2**—Demonstrate command of standard English **capitalization**, **punctuation**, and spelling.
3–5	parts of speech	**Language Anchor Standard 3.2**—Demonstrate command of standard English grammar and usage when writing or **speaking**.
6	spelling	**Language Anchor Standard 3.2**—Demonstrate command of standard English capitalization, punctuation, and **spelling**.

Note: Because articles and possessive pronouns are also adjectives, they are included in the answer key as such. Depending on students' knowledge of this, grade activity sheets accordingly.

HOW TO USE THIS BOOK *(cont.)*

Using the Practice Pages

Practice pages provide instruction and assessment opportunities for each day of the school year. Teachers may wish to prepare packets of weekly practice pages for the classroom or for homework. As outlined on page 5, every question is aligned to a language skill.

Practice pages provide instruction and assessment opportunities for each day of the school year.

Each question ties student practice to a specific language skill.

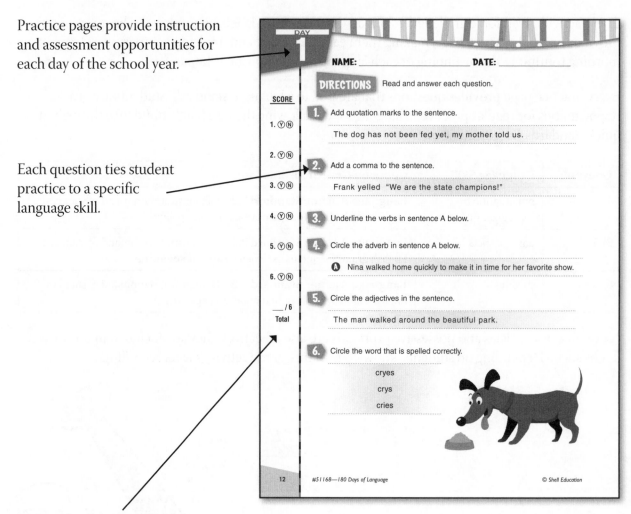

Using the Scoring Guide

Use the scoring guide along the side of each practice page to check answers and see at a glance which skills may need more reinforcement.

Fill in the appropriate circle for each problem to indicate correct (Y) or incorrect (N) responses. You might wish to indicate only incorrect responses to focus on those skills. (For example, if students consistently miss items 2 and 4, they may need additional help with those concepts as outlined in the table on page 5.) Use the answer key at the back of the book to score the problems, or you may call out answers to have students self-score or peer-score their work.

HOW TO USE THIS BOOK (cont.)

Diagnostic Assessment

Teachers can use the practice pages as diagnostic assessments. The data analysis tools included with the book enable teachers or parents to quickly score students' work and monitor their progress. Teachers and parents can see at a glance which language skills students may need to target in order to develop proficiency.

After students complete a practice page, grade each page using the answer key (pages 192–206). Then, complete the *Practice Page Item Analysis* for the appropriate day (page 8) for the whole class, or the *Student Item Analysis* (page 9) for individual students. These charts are also provided on the Digital Resource CD as PDFs, Microsoft Word® files, and as Microsoft Excel® files (filenames: pageitem.pdf, pageitem.doc, pageitem.xls; studentitem.pdf, studentitem.doc, studentitem.xls). Teachers can input data into the electronic files directly on the computer, or they can print the pages and analyze students' work using paper and pencil.

To complete the Practice Page Item Analyses:

- Write or type students' names in the far-left column. Depending on the number of students, more than one copy of the form may be needed, or you may need to add rows.

- The item numbers are included across the top of the chart. Each item correlates with the matching question number from the practice page.

- For each student, record an *X* in the column if the student has the item incorrect. If the item is correct, leave the space in the column blank.

- If you are using the Excel file, totals will be automatically generated. If you are using the Word file or if you have printed the PDF, you will need to compute the totals. Count the *X*s in each row and column and fill in the correct boxes.

To complete the Student Item Analyses:

- Write or type the student's name on the top row. This form tracks the ongoing progress of each student, so one copy per student is necessary.

- The item numbers are included across the top of the chart. Each item correlates with the matching question number from the practice page.

- For each day, record an *X* in the column if the student has the item incorrect. If the item is correct, leave the space in the column blank.

- If you are using the Excel file, totals will be automatically generated. If you are using the Word file or if you have printed the PDF, you will need to compute the totals. Count the *X*s in each row and column and fill in the correct boxes.

HOW TO USE THIS BOOK (cont.)

Practice Page Item Analysis

Directions: Record an *X* in cells to indicate where students have missed questions. Add up the totals. You can view: (1) which questions/concepts were missed per student; (2) the total correct score for each student; and (3) the total number of students who missed each question.

Day: _____ / _____ Question # Student Name	1	2	3	4	5	6	# correct
Sample Student		x			x	x	**3/6**
# of students missing each question							

HOW TO USE THIS BOOK *(cont.)*

Student Item Analysis

Directions: Record an *X* in cells to indicate where the student has missed questions. Add up the totals. You can view: (1) which questions/concepts the student missed; (2) the total correct score per day; and (3) the total number of times each question/concept was missed.

Student Name: Sample Student							
Question	**1**	**2**	**3**	**4**	**5**	**6**	**# correct**
Day							
1		X			X		4/6
Total							

HOW TO USE THIS BOOK *(cont.)*

Using the Results to Differentiate Instruction

Once results are gathered and analyzed, teachers can use the results to inform the way they differentiate instruction. The data can help determine which concepts are the most difficult for students and which need additional instructional support and continued practice. Depending on how often the practice pages are scored, results can be considered for instructional support on a daily or weekly basis.

Whole-Class Support

The results of the diagnostic analysis may show that the entire class is struggling with a particular concept or group of concepts. If these concepts have been taught in the past, this indicates that further instruction or reteaching is necessary. If these concepts have not been taught in the past, this data is a great preassessment and may demonstrate that students do not have a working knowledge of the concepts. Thus, careful planning for the length of the unit(s) or lesson(s) must be considered, and additional front-loading may be required.

Small-Group or Individual Support

The results of the diagnostic analysis may show that an individual or a small group of students is struggling with a particular concept or group of concepts. If these concepts have been taught in the past, this indicates that further instruction or reteaching is necessary. Consider pulling aside these students while others are working independently to instruct further on the concept(s). Teachers can also use the results to help identify individuals or groups of proficient students who are ready for enrichment or above-grade-level instruction. These students may benefit from independent learning contracts or more challenging activities. Students may also benefit from extra practice using games or computer-based resources.

Digital Resource CD

The Digital Resource CD provides the following resources:

- Standards Correlations Chart

- Reproducible PDFs of each practice page

- Directions for completing the diagnostic Item Analysis forms

- *Practice Page Item Analysis* PDFs, Word documents, and Excel spreadsheets

- *Student Item Analysis* PDFs, Word documents, and Excel spreadsheets

STANDARDS CORRELATIONS

Shell Education is committed to producing educational materials that are research and standards based. In this effort, we have correlated all of our products to the academic standards of all 50 states, the District of Columbia, the Department of Defense Dependents Schools, and all Canadian provinces.

How to Find Standards Correlations

To print a customized correlation report of this product for your state, visit our website at http://www.shelleducation.com and follow the on-screen directions. If you require assistance in printing correlation reports, please contact our Customer Service Department at 1-877-777-3450.

Purpose and Intent of Standards

Legislation mandates that all states adopt academic standards that identify the skills students will learn in kindergarten through grade twelve. Many states also have standards for Pre–K. This same legislation sets requirements to ensure the standards are detailed and comprehensive.

Standards are designed to focus instruction and guide adoption of curricula. Standards are statements that describe the criteria necessary for students to meet specific academic goals. They define the knowledge, skills, and content students should acquire at each level. Standards are also used to develop standardized tests to evaluate students' academic progress. Teachers are required to demonstrate how their lessons meet state standards. State standards are used in the development of all of our products, so educators can be assured they meet the academic requirements of each state.

Common Core State Standards

The activities in this book are aligned to the Common Core State Standards (CCSS). The chart on page 5 lists the anchor standards. The chart is also on the Digital Resource CD (filename: standards.pdf).

NAME: _____ **DATE:** _____

DIRECTIONS Read and answer each question.

1. Y N

1. Add quotation marks to the sentence.

The dog has not been fed yet, my mother told us.

2. Y N

2. Add a comma to the sentence.

3. Y N

Frank yelled "We are the state champions!"

4. Y N

3. Underline the verbs in sentence A below.

5. Y N

4. Circle the adverb in sentence A below.

A Nina walked home quickly to make it in time for her favorite show.

6. Y N

5. Circle the adjectives in the sentence.

The man walked around the beautiful park.

___ / 6
Total

6. Circle the word that is spelled correctly.

cryes

crys

cries

NAME: _____ **DATE:** _____

DIRECTIONS Read and answer each question.

1. Add a comma to the following address.

1700 Lakeview Place

Springfield OR 99810

2. Rewrite the book title <u>the zookeeper's job</u> using correct capitalization.

_____

3. Write a sentence using the noun *bravery*.

_____

_____

4. Write the correct verb to complete the sentence.

When my teacher got angry with me, I _____ embarrassed.

(felt, felted, feel)

5. Circle the pronoun in the sentence.

Mr. Jackson told his class that there was an assembly.

6. Write the correctly spelled word to complete the sentence.

The dancer _____ her shoes quickly to the beat.

(taped, tapped, tappet)

1. Ⓨ Ⓝ

2. Ⓨ Ⓝ

3. Ⓨ Ⓝ

4. Ⓨ Ⓝ

5. Ⓨ Ⓝ

6. Ⓨ Ⓝ

___ / 6
Total

NAME: _____ **DATE:** _____

DIRECTIONS Read and answer each question.

1. Write your address. Be sure to include a comma.

_____

_____

2. Rewrite the song title "bicycle built for two" using correct capitalization.

_____

3. Rewrite sentence A below in the past tense.

_____

_____

4. Rewrite sentence A below in the future tense.

_____

_____

A I walk to school every day.

5. Write the correct verb to complete the sentence.

I watched the red leaf _____ from the oak tree.
(fall, fell, fallen)

6. Which word is spelled correctly?

writeng   writing   writeing

#51168—180 Days of Language

NAME: _____ **DATE:** _____

DIRECTIONS Read and answer each question.

1. Add quotation marks to the sentence.

I don't want to have salad for dinner, moaned Jeremy.

2. Add a comma to the sentence.

"I want to go see the parade downtown " said Gus.

3. Circle the adjectives in the sentence.

Our big, brown, furry dog sheds and leaves hair everywhere.

4. An **abstract noun** is a noun that cannot be identified using the five senses. Circle the abstract noun in the sentence.

I have some knowledge about the rules of tennis.

5. What is the plural of *man*?

man's   mans   men

6. Which word correctly adds the *-ness* suffix?

weakeness   happiness   playfullness

NAME: _____ **DATE:** _____

DIRECTIONS Read and answer each question.

1. Add quotation marks to the sentence.

Please don't take anything out of my desk, Paul said.

2. Add quotation marks to the sentence.

Where should we go for dinner tonight? wondered Alice.

3. Write the correct adjective to complete the sentence.

Our music teacher is the _____ teacher I have ever had.
(nice, nicer, nicest)

4. Write the correct adverb to complete the sentence.

I mow the lawn _____ than my brother.
(often, more often, most often)

5. Which is the correct plural word?

sheep   sheeps   sheepes

6. Circle the word that is spelled correctly.

acktion   funktion   motion

NAME: _____ DATE: _____

DIRECTIONS Read and answer each question.

1. Add an apostrophe to the sentence.

Henrys dog likes to run.

2. Add a comma to the following address.

12 Hancock Avenue

Princeville FL 65291

3. Combine the sentences. Include the word *but.*

Doreen wants to go to the baseball game. She also wants to go swimming.

_____

_____

4. Write a sentence using the noun *childhood.*

_____

_____

5. Circle the pronoun in the sentence.

Mrs. Burns wanted to share her pictures with the class.

6. Circle the word that is spelled correctly.

droppt   droped   dropped

NAME: _____ **DATE:** _____

DIRECTIONS Read and answer each question.

SCORE

1. Ⓨ Ⓝ

2. Ⓨ Ⓝ

3. Ⓨ Ⓝ

4. Ⓨ Ⓝ

5. Ⓨ Ⓝ

6. Ⓨ Ⓝ

___ / 6
Total

1. Rewrite the sentence using an apostrophe.

The book belonging to Frances was due today at the library.

_____

_____

2. Add quotation marks and a comma to the sentence.

Here is the book I was telling you about   said Heather.

3. Circle the conjunction in the sentence.

We can have silent reading time, or we can have partner reading time.

4. Write the correct adjective to complete the sentence.

I think that strawberries are _____ than bananas.
(sweet, sweeter, sweetest)

5. Add an adverb to complete the sentence.

The ant moved _____ across the ground.

6. Circle the word that is spelled correctly.

spoting   spoteing   spotting

NAME: _____ **DATE:** _____

DIRECTIONS Read and answer each question.

1. Rewrite *the friend of José* in another way.

_____

1. Ⓨ Ⓝ

2. Ⓨ Ⓝ

2. Add a comma to the following address.

723 Pine Road

Grant Falls GA 09221

3. Ⓨ Ⓝ

3. Circle the conjunction in the sentence.

The librarian wanted to help, yet the child was fine on her own.

4. Ⓨ Ⓝ

5. Ⓨ Ⓝ

4. Write the correct adverb to complete the sentence.

Jesse walked in the library _____
than Kira did.   (quietly, more quietly, most quietly)

6. Ⓨ Ⓝ

___ / 6
Total

5. Add a verb to the sentence.

Elephants _____ as they travel across the land as a herd.

6. Circle the word that is spelled correctly.

needet   neded   needed

NAME: _____ **DATE:** _____

DIRECTIONS Read and answer each question.

1. Y N

1. Rewrite the sentence using an apostrophe.

The mother of Lily wanted to drive on the field trip.

2. Y N

_____

_____

3. Y N

2. Circle another way to write *the chair belonging to my teacher*.

4. Y N

my teachers chair   my teachers' chair   my teacher's chair

5. Y N

3. Circle the conjunction in the sentence.

6. Y N

Reehan wants to play soccer, so he asked his friends to play.

___ / 6
Total

4. Write the correct adverb to complete the sentence.

Sam buys lunch _____ because he likes the cafeteria's
food.   (often, most often)

5. Circle the verb that *slowly* describes.

Chloe dressed slowly in the morning before school.

6. Circle the word that is spelled correctly.

lateley   latly   lately

NAME: _____ **DATE:** _____

DIRECTIONS Read and answer each question.

1. Write *the bike belonging to Evan* in another way.

_____

2. Add a comma to the following address.

11 Veneto Road
Virginia City VA 75400

3. Circle the adjectives in the sentence.

Oliver liked blue cotton candy and red licorice.

4. Circle the word that is the past tense of *begin*.

begined   beginning   began

5. Rewrite the following sentence in the past tense.

I will move to a new home and start a new school.

_____

_____

6. Circle the word that is spelled correctly.

really   realy   realley

NAME: _____ **DATE:** _____

DIRECTIONS Read and answer each question.

1. Circle the words in the sentence that need capital letters.

I wanted to read <u>a princess tale</u>, which is the sequel book <u>to the castle in the sky</u>.

2. Add a comma to the following address.

4439 Parkson Road

Bridgetown NH 45200

3. Write a sentence using the noun *adventure*.

_____

_____

4. Circle the adjectives in the sentence.

The loud noises were coming from the busy nest.

5. Circle the word that is the past tense of *have*.

haved   havt   had

6. Circle the word that is spelled correctly.

briteness   brightness   brightniss

NAME: _____ DATE: _____

DIRECTIONS Read and answer each question.

1. Write the title of your favorite book using correct capitalization.

_____

2. Add quotation marks to the sentence.

I cannot wait for the school play tomorrow, said Ava.

3. Rewrite sentence A below in the past tense.

_____

_____

4. Rewrite sentence A below in the future tense.

_____

_____

Ⓐ I write in my journal every day.

5. Rewrite the sentence using the correct pronoun.

Mona said that his dinner portion was too big to eat.

_____

_____

6. Circle the word that is spelled correctly.

finding   fynding   findeing

NAME: _____ **DATE:** _____

DIRECTIONS Read and answer each question.

1. Write titles using correct capitalization.

1. Ⓨ Ⓝ

Book Title: _____

Movie Title: _____

2. Ⓨ Ⓝ

2. Add quotation marks and a comma to the sentence.

3. Ⓨ Ⓝ

The birthday party is going to start on time   said Paulina.

4. Ⓨ Ⓝ

3. Circle the pronoun in the sentence.

5. Ⓨ Ⓝ

Kay wanted to pack her own lunch.

6. Ⓨ Ⓝ

4. Write the correct adjective to complete the sentence.

___ / 6
Total

Some breeds of dogs are _____ than other breeds.
(smart, smarter, smartest)

5. What does the adjective *blue* describe in the sentence?

When I look at the gorgeous ocean, all I can see is the clear, blue water.

_____

6. Circle the word that is spelled correctly.

bushs   bushs'   bushes

NAME: _____ DATE: _____

DIRECTIONS Read and answer each question.

1. Add an apostrophe to the sentence.

Stephanies brother was not behaving at dinner.

1. Ⓨ Ⓝ

2. Add quotation marks and a comma to the sentence.

That music is making my head hurt   Francisco complained.

2. Ⓨ Ⓝ

3. Ⓨ Ⓝ

3. Write the correct verb to complete the sentence.

Christmas _____ not on a weekend this year.
(is, are, were)

4. Ⓨ Ⓝ

5. Ⓨ Ⓝ

4. Circle the verb in the sentence.

The candle burned all night long.

6. Ⓨ Ⓝ

___ / 6
Total

5. Rewrite the sentence using the correct pronoun.

My sister never wants to share his toys with me.

_____

_____

6. Circle the word that is spelled correctly.

benches   benchs   benchus

NAME: _____ DATE: _____

DIRECTIONS Read and answer each question.

1. Ⓨ Ⓝ

1. Add an apostrophe to the sentence.

I don't know where Lucys library book might be.

2. Ⓨ Ⓝ

2. Add quotation marks to the sentence.

Lucas shouted, Let's run out to the playground before anyone else!

3. Ⓨ Ⓝ

3. Write a sentence using the noun *communication.*

4. Ⓨ Ⓝ

5. Ⓨ Ⓝ

_____

_____

6. Ⓨ Ⓝ

4. Write the correct verb to complete the sentence.

___ / 6
Total

A kangaroo _____ a pouch on its stomach for carrying its baby.   (have, has, had)

5. Circle the adjectives in the sentence.

The brown horse galloped along the sandy beach.

6. Circle the word that is spelled correctly.

trax   tracks   traks

NAME: _____ DATE: _____

DIRECTIONS Read and answer each question.

1. Rewrite the sentence using an apostrophe.

The friend of Jason was trying to organize a kickball game.

_____

_____

1. Ⓨ Ⓝ

2. Ⓨ Ⓝ

2. Add quotation marks and a comma to the sentence.

My mom will buy us pizza at the party   Charlie explained.

3. Ⓨ Ⓝ

4. Ⓨ Ⓝ

3. Write the correct verb to complete the sentence.

The second graders _____ nervous about their
performance today.   (is, are, was)

5. Ⓨ Ⓝ

6. Ⓨ Ⓝ

4. Circle the adjectives in the sentence.

The large fish is looking for smaller fish to eat.

___ / 6
Total

5. Circle the plural noun in the sentence.

People visited the zoo today.

6. Circle the word that is spelled correctly.

berry   berre   berrie

NAME: _____ **DATE:** _____

| DIRECTIONS | Read and answer each question. |

1. Ⓨ Ⓝ

2. Ⓨ Ⓝ

3. Ⓨ Ⓝ

4. Ⓨ Ⓝ

5. Ⓨ Ⓝ

6. Ⓨ Ⓝ

___ / 6
Total

1. Rewrite the sentence using an apostrophe.

The lunch box belonging to Ted was in the lost and found.

_____

_____

2. Add quotation marks and a comma to the sentence.

Gus explained   I was late for school because the alarm did not go off.

3. Write a sentence using the noun *honesty.*

_____

_____

4. Many plural nouns end in *-s* or *-es*. Circle the noun that does **not** follow this rule.

wish   foot   house

5. Circle the proper noun.

Where should Mary go to walk her dog on a trail?

6. Circle the word that is spelled correctly.

muddie   mudde   muddy

NAME: _____ **DATE:** _____

| DIRECTIONS | Read and answer each question. |

1. Write *the dog belonging to Rita* in another way.

_____

1. Ⓨ Ⓝ

2. Add a comma to the address.

....
1650 Warner Road

New York NY 12112
....

2. Ⓨ Ⓝ

3. Ⓨ Ⓝ

3. Circle the adjectives.

....
Principal Parker has unruly students in her office.
....

4. Ⓨ Ⓝ

5. Ⓨ Ⓝ

4. Circle the word that represents past tense.

....
Pablo played soccer in the championship game.
....

6. Ⓨ Ⓝ

___ / 6
Total

5. Write the correct adjective to complete the sentence.

....

Mom was _____ than Dad at the mess.
             (angry, angrier, angriest)

....

6. Circle the word that is spelled correctly.

....
      smiled

      smild

      smiyeled
....

NAME: _____ **DATE:** _____

DIRECTIONS Read and answer each question.

1. (Y)(N)

1. Write *the baby brother of Hector* in another way.

_____

2. (Y)(N)

2. Write the address of your school. Be sure to include a comma.

_____

3. (Y)(N)

_____

4. (Y)(N)

3. Circle the verbs in the sentence.

The baby bird has to find its way to the nest.

5. (Y)(N)

4. Rewrite the sentence using the correct pronouns.

6. (Y)(N)

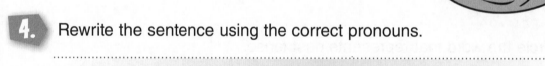

Mom watched Henry to make sure she was playing nicely with her friend.

___ / 6
Total

_____

_____

5. Circle the words that represent past tense.

Oliver did not want to go to the dentist because he was scared.

6. Circle the word that is spelled correctly.

matchs   matches   maches

NAME: _____ **DATE:** _____

DIRECTIONS Read and answer each question.

1. Write *the birthday party of Desi* in another way.

_____

1. Ⓨ Ⓝ

2. Add apostrophes to the sentence.

Jacobs aunt was not able to bring Jacobs cousin to the party.

2. Ⓨ Ⓝ

3. Ⓨ Ⓝ

3. Rewrite the sentence in the past tense.

The lake will dry up because there will not be enough rain this season.

_____

_____

4. Ⓨ Ⓝ

5. Ⓨ Ⓝ

6. Ⓨ Ⓝ

4. Circle the adverb in the sentence.

The field trip happened so quickly that it surprised me when it was over.

___ / 6
Total

5. Circle the pronoun in the sentence.

Violet's father used his own flashlight on the camping trip.

6. Circle the word that is spelled correctly.

richis   riches   richs

NAME: _____ **DATE:** _____

DIRECTIONS Read and answer each question.

1. (Y)(N)

1. Write *the tooth belonging to Roman* in another way.

_____

2. (Y)(N)

2. Add a comma to the following address.

544 Hancock Lane

3. (Y)(N)

West Franklin IL 68221

4. (Y)(N)

3. Circle the verbs in the sentence.

5. (Y)(N)

Bagels are not my favorite food to eat for breakfast.

6. (Y)(N)

4. Write a sentence using the word *sympathy*.

_____

___ / 6
Total

_____

5. Circle the word that is the past tense of *buy*.

buying   buyed   bought

6. Circle the word that is spelled correctly.

happen

hapen

happin

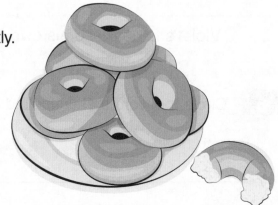

NAME: _____ DATE: _____

DIRECTIONS Read and answer each question.

1. Add a comma to the following address.

1812 Harding Court

Clayton PA 98850

1. Ⓨ Ⓝ

2. Ⓨ Ⓝ

2. Add quotation marks and a comma to the sentence.

Hank commented   I wish that I could have a cupcake.

3. Ⓨ Ⓝ

3. Write a sentence using the word *curiosity*.

_____

_____

4. Ⓨ Ⓝ

5. Ⓨ Ⓝ

4. Circle the adverb in the sentence.

The sea turtle waddled slowly across the beach.

6. Ⓨ Ⓝ

___ / 6
Total

5. Circle the adjectives in the sentence.

My excited dog wants to go to the park.

6. Circle the word that is spelled correctly.

swiming

swimming

swiminng

NAME: _____ **DATE:** _____

SCORE

1. Ⓨ Ⓝ

2. Ⓨ Ⓝ

3. Ⓨ Ⓝ

4. Ⓨ Ⓝ

5. Ⓨ Ⓝ

6. Ⓨ Ⓝ

___ / 6
Total

DIRECTIONS Read and answer each question.

1. Write *the tire on the car* in another way.

_____

2. Add quotation marks and a comma to the sentence.

I like to drink my tea while it is hot   Grandma explained.

3. Write the correct verb to complete the sentence.

All insects _____ three body parts.
(have, has, had)

4. Circle the nouns in the sentence.

Tomorrow, I will remember to bring my homework to school.

5. Combine the sentences. Include the word *or*.

I can order cheese pizza. I can order pepperoni pizza.

_____

_____

6. Circle the word that is spelled correctly.

unclear   inclear   uncleer

NAME: _____ **DATE:** _____

DIRECTIONS Read and answer each question.

1. Write *the picture on the map* in another way.

_____

1. Ⓨ Ⓝ

2. Circle the words that need to be capitalized.

The librarian found me the book that I wanted, titled <u>abe lincoln's boyhood</u>.

2. Ⓨ Ⓝ

3. Ⓨ Ⓝ

3. Write the correct adverb to complete the sentence.

Frank practices football _____ so that he can play for the competitive team.   (often, most often)

4. Ⓨ Ⓝ

5. Ⓨ Ⓝ

4. Circle the conjunction in the sentence.

The waves were getting higher, so we decided to stop swimming in the ocean.

6. Ⓨ Ⓝ

_____ / 6
Total

5. Circle the correct word that is the past tense of *shake*.

shaked   shaking   shook

6. Circle the word that is spelled correctly.

aganst   against   agenst

NAME: _____ DATE: _____

DIRECTIONS   Read and answer each question.

1. Add a comma to the following address.

1. Ⓨ Ⓝ

12 Brookhurst

West Covington KY 29930

2. Ⓨ Ⓝ

2. Add an apostrophe to the sentence.

3. Ⓨ Ⓝ

Jacks mom was not able to help us with our homework, so we worked together.

4. Ⓨ Ⓝ

3. Write the correct pronoun to complete the sentence.

5. Ⓨ Ⓝ

Sally loves to play with _____ dog at the park.
                        (their, his, her)

6. Ⓨ Ⓝ

4. Circle the adverb in the sentence.

___/6
Total

John got up angrily and stormed out of the room after an argument.

5. Write the past tense of the word *get* in the blank.

Yesterday was the day I _____ a new bike.

6. Circle the word that is spelled correctly.

erupped   eruped   erupt

NAME: _____ DATE: _____

DIRECTIONS Read and answer each question.

1. Circle the words in the sentence that need capital letters.

My friend recommends reading <u>the mystery solver</u> by Hank Williams.

1. Ⓨ Ⓝ

2. Ⓨ Ⓝ

2. Add quotation marks and a comma to the sentence.

All of our animals have been rescued by our staff   explained the zookeeper.

3. Ⓨ Ⓝ

4. Ⓨ Ⓝ

3. Write the correct verb to complete the sentence.

The giraffe _____ reaching for leaves in the tall tree.
(is, are, were)

5. Ⓨ Ⓝ

6. Ⓨ Ⓝ

4. Combine the sentences. Include the word *but*.

The school day was over. The bus was still not there.

_____

_____

___ / 6
Total

5. Circle the plural nouns in the sentence.

The dentist looked at my teeth to check for cavities.

6. Circle the word that is spelled correctly.

stitch   stich   stiche

NAME: _____ DATE: _____

DIRECTIONS Read and answer each question.

SCORE

1. Write *the barbecue that belongs to Michael* in another way.

1. Ⓨ Ⓝ

_____

2. Ⓨ Ⓝ

2. Use an apostrophe to write *the work of Mr. Franklin* in another way.

_____

3. Ⓨ Ⓝ

.

3. Write a sentence using the word *success*.

4. Ⓨ Ⓝ

_____

_____

5. Ⓨ Ⓝ

4. Many plural nouns end in *-s* or *-es*. Circle the noun that does **not** follow this rule.

6. Ⓨ Ⓝ

broom   stick   sheep

___ / 6
Total

5. Circle the adverb in the sentence.

The kitten playfully swatted the ball of yarn.

6. Circle the word that is spelled correctly.

crawl

crowl

krawl

NAME: _____ DATE: _____

SCORE

1. Circle the words that need capital letters.

1. Ⓨ Ⓝ

The radio just played my favorite song, "missing you."

2. Ⓨ Ⓝ

2. Add a comma to the following address.

701 Kenton Road

Berkeley CA 88720

3. Ⓨ Ⓝ

4. Ⓨ Ⓝ

3. Circle the adverb in the sentence.

The truck sped quickly down the highway.

5. Ⓨ Ⓝ

4. What are adverbs?

6. Ⓨ Ⓝ

_____

_____

___ / 6

Total

5. Write the correct adjective to complete the sentence.

Polly wanted to be wearing the _____ dress in the group.
(fancy, fancier, fanciest)

6. Circle the word that is spelled correctly.

hoter   hotter   hawter

NAME: _____ **DATE:** _____

DIRECTIONS Read and answer each question.

1. Ⓨ Ⓝ

2. Ⓨ Ⓝ

3. Ⓨ Ⓝ

4. Ⓨ Ⓝ

5. Ⓨ Ⓝ

6. Ⓨ Ⓝ

___ / 6
Total

1. Write *the video game belonging to Roberto* in another way.

_____

2. Add quotation marks and an exclamation point to the sentence.

Our family gathering was a lot of fun   Anna exclaimed.

3. Rewrite the sentence using the correct pronoun.

The mother bear was trying to take care of his cubs.

_____

_____

4. Write two adjectives that describe your school.

_____   _____

5. Combine the sentences. Include the word *and*.

The snow was falling all day. The neighborhood was quiet.

_____

_____

6. Circle the word that is spelled correctly.

sadest   saddest   saddist

NAME: _____ DATE: _____

DIRECTIONS Read and answer each question.

1. Circle the words that need to be capitalized.

1. Ⓨ Ⓝ

I read the poem "gray day at the beach," aloud to the class.

2. Ⓨ Ⓝ

2. Add a comma to the following address.

3. Ⓨ Ⓝ

229 Adams Road

West Palm Beach FL 88720

4. Ⓨ Ⓝ

3. Use the word *generosity* in a sentence.

5. Ⓨ Ⓝ

_____

_____

6. Ⓨ Ⓝ

4. Circle the pronouns in the sentence.

___ / 6
Total

Dad and I decided to ride our bikes on the trail.

5. Combine the sentences. Include the word *but*.

Mom wanted to take all of the kids to the beach. It was raining.

_____

_____

6. Circle the word that is spelled correctly.

knight   knite   knighte

NAME: _____ **DATE:** _____

SCORE

DIRECTIONS Read and answer each question.

1. Write the name of the place you live in using correct capitalization.

1. Ⓨ Ⓝ

_____

2. Use an apostrophe to write *the lunch that belongs to Oscar* in another way.

2. Ⓨ Ⓝ

3. Ⓨ Ⓝ

_____

3. Write a sentence using the word *imagination*.

4. Ⓨ Ⓝ

_____

5. Ⓨ Ⓝ

_____

4. Circle the adjectives in the sentence.

6. Ⓨ Ⓝ

The green grass grew quickly under the warm sun.

___ / 6
Total

5. Write the plural noun to complete the sentence.

The _____ swim through the water for food.
(shark)

6. Circle the word that is spelled correctly.

shortly

shortley

shortlie

NAME: _____ **DATE:** _____

DIRECTIONS Read and answer each question.

SCORE

1. Circle the words that need capital letters.

1. Ⓨ Ⓝ

My favorite movie is titled *beauty and the beast*.

2. Ⓨ Ⓝ

2. Add quotation marks and an exclamation point to the sentence.

3. Ⓨ Ⓝ

The video was a lot of fun to make   Kevin exclaimed.

3. Combine the sentences. Include the word *before.*

4. Ⓨ Ⓝ

I go to school. I eat my breakfast.

5. Ⓨ Ⓝ

_____

6. Ⓨ Ⓝ

_____

4. Write the correct adjective to complete the sentence.

___ / 6

Total

The green salsa was much _____ than the red salsa.
(hot, hotter, hottest)

5. Circle the adverb in the sentence.

The boys played happily and built a fort with the pillows.

6. Circle the word that is spelled correctly.

changing   changeing   chanjing

NAME: _____ **DATE:** _____

SCORE

DIRECTIONS   Read and answer each question.

1. Circle the words that need capital letters.

1. (Y)(N)

I have been wondering if the title <u>a doomsday mystery</u> means the book will be scary.

2. (Y)(N)

2. Add an apostrophe to the sentence.

3. (Y)(N)

Heathers homework was not inside her backpack.

4. (Y)(N)

3. Combine the sentences. Include the word *and*.

5. (Y)(N)

Leslie played on the playground. Her mom came to get her.

_____

6. (Y)(N)

_____

___ / 6
Total

4. Fill in the blanks with nouns.

A _____ is smaller than a _____.

5. Fill in the blank with a verb.

A mouse _____ up a tree.

6. Circle the word that is spelled correctly.

leaves   leavs   leavez

NAME: _____ **DATE:** _____

DIRECTIONS Read and answer each question.

1. Add quotation marks and a comma to the sentence.

Lin wondered   Why has our teacher been absent all week?

1. Ⓨ Ⓝ

2. Use an apostrophe to write *the petal on the flower* in another way.

_____

2. Ⓨ Ⓝ

3. Ⓨ Ⓝ

3. Write the correct verb to complete the sentence.

My pet guinea pig _____ right
out of my hand.   (eat, eats, eating)

4. Ⓨ Ⓝ

4. Write a sentence using the noun *courage*.

_____

_____

5. Ⓨ Ⓝ

6. Ⓨ Ⓝ

____ / 6
Total

5. Write two adjectives to complete the sentence.

The _____, _____ sky was
a beautiful sight from the top of the mountain.

6. Circle the word that is spelled correctly.

mainley   mainlie   mainly

NAME: _____ **DATE:** _____

DIRECTIONS Read and answer each question.

SCORE

1. Ⓨ Ⓝ

2. Ⓨ Ⓝ

3. Ⓨ Ⓝ

4. Ⓨ Ⓝ

5. Ⓨ Ⓝ

6. Ⓨ Ⓝ

___ / 6
Total

1. Add quotation marks and a comma to the sentence.

Please do not eat food in the museum   the employee warned the students.

2. Add an apostrophe to the sentence.

Jacksons sister was always following us around.

3. Circle the pronouns in the sentence.

Sophia wanted to take her backpack with her on the trip.

4. Circle the adverb in the sentence.

The airplane landed safely after a rough ride.

5. Rewrite the sentence in the present tense.

Mean kids at the playground acted like bullies and teased us.

_____

_____

6. Circle the word that is spelled correctly.

halvez   halfs   halves

NAME: _____ **DATE:** _____

DIRECTIONS Read and answer each question.

1. Circle the words in the sentence that need capital letters.

I think I may sing the song titled "a starry night" for the talent show.

2. Use an apostrophe to write *the pockets in the coat* in another way.

_____

3. Circle the words that represent the past tense.

The family strolled on the beach and looked for shells.

4. Circle the adjectives in the sentence.

I heard the speeding car race down our quiet street.

5. Combine the sentences. Include the word *since.*

The weather is nice. I can go swimming outside.

_____

_____

6. Circle the word that is spelled correctly.

placemint

placement

plasement

1. Ⓨ Ⓝ

2. Ⓨ Ⓝ

3. Ⓨ Ⓝ

4. Ⓨ Ⓝ

5. Ⓨ Ⓝ

6. Ⓨ Ⓝ

___ / 6
Total

NAME: _____ DATE: _____

DIRECTIONS Read and answer each question.

1. (Y) (N)

1. Circle the words in the sentence that need capital letters.

The radio station always plays the song titled "feeling silly and funky."

2. (Y) (N)

2. Add an apostrophe to the sentence.

My neighbors swimming pool felt very refreshing on a hot day.

3. (Y) (N)

3. Rewrite the sentence using the correct pronoun.

My uncle flew into town and brought two suitcases with her.

4. (Y) (N)

_____

5. (Y) (N)

_____

6. (Y) (N)

___ / 6
Total

4. Many plural nouns end in -s or -es. Circle the noun that does **not** follow this rule.

      cat   man   table

5. Write a sentence using the verb *trust* in it.

_____

_____

6. Circle the word that is spelled correctly.

      aging   ajing   ageing

NAME: _____ DATE: _____

DIRECTIONS Read and answer each question.

1. Add a comma to the following address.

80 Broadway Avenue

Parklane MT 68868

2. Use an apostrophe to write *the ring around the planet* in another way.

_____

3. Rewrite the sentence using the correct pronoun.

The driver got in his car and drove to her mom's house.

_____

_____

4. Circle the transition word in the sentence.

Dogs like to eat, although they should not eat a lot of human food.

5. Write the correct verb to complete the sentence.

The tarantula _____ slowly across the sand.
(moves, move, moving)

6. Circle the word that is spelled correctly.

larjer   largure   larger

1. Ⓨ Ⓝ

2. Ⓨ Ⓝ

3. Ⓨ Ⓝ

4. Ⓨ Ⓝ

5. Ⓨ Ⓝ

6. Ⓨ Ⓝ

___ / 6
Total

NAME: _____ **DATE:** _____

SCORE

1. Ⓨ Ⓝ

2. Ⓨ Ⓝ

3. Ⓨ Ⓝ

4. Ⓨ Ⓝ

5. Ⓨ Ⓝ

6. Ⓨ Ⓝ

___ / 6
Total

DIRECTIONS Read and answer each question.

1. Add a comma to the following address.

1220 Irving Lane

Santa Maria CA 99093

2. Use an apostrophe to write *the cub belonging to the black bear* in another way.

_____

3. Write the correct verb to complete the sentence.

A telescope _____ people see things that are far away.
(helps, help, helping)

4. Write two adverbs to complete the sentence.

The butterfly flew _____ and _____ through the sky.

5. Write a sentence using the word *wisdom* in it.

_____

_____

6. Circle the word that is spelled correctly.

worry   worrie   worre

NAME: _____ **DATE:** _____

> **DIRECTIONS** Read and answer each question.

1. Add a comma to the following address.

14 Grant Court

Highland CO 75900

2. Add an apostrophe to the sentence.

Joshuas story was written in a week during writing time.

3. Rewrite the sentence using the correct pronoun.

He likes to ride her skateboard to school.

_____

_____

4. Circle the adverb in the sentence.

The bus driver greets me cheerfully every morning at the bus stop.

5. Write the correct adjective to complete the sentence.

Based on weight, the brown puppy is the _____ dog in the litter. (small, smaller, smallest)

6. Circle the word that is spelled correctly.

hurrie   hurre   hurry

NAME: _____ DATE: _____

DIRECTIONS Read and answer each question.

1. Circle the words in the sentence that need capital letters.

Should we dance to the song "party people" or the song "from my heart"?

2. Add a comma to the sentence.

I am looking for the hotel in Paris France.

3. Rewrite the sentence in the future tense.

The students from Parker School are picking up litter.

_____

_____

4. Circle the adjectives in the sentence.

A healthy sunflower plant continued to grow green leaves.

5. Circle the plural noun in the sentence.

Maria's mom reads a lot of books.

6. Add an -ed ending to the base word *plan*. Write the word on the line.

_____

NAME: _____ DATE: _____

DIRECTIONS Read and answer each question.

1. Circle the words that need capital letters.

....

The books <u>over the deep end</u> and <u>under the bridge</u> are both written by the same author.

....

2. Add a comma to the sentence.

....

Santiago is trying to save money to visit his family in Albuquerque New Mexico.

....

3. Rewrite the sentence in past tense.

....

The fly buzzes around the kitchen.

_____

_____

....

4. Many plural nouns end in -*s* or -*es*. Circle the noun that does **not** follow this rule.

....

    book   computer   child

....

5. Circle the adverb.

....

The zookeeper excitedly shared facts about the zoo's new lions.

....

6. Add a -*ness* ending to the base word *happy*. Write the word on the line.

_____

1. Ⓨ Ⓝ

2. Ⓨ Ⓝ

3. Ⓨ Ⓝ

4. Ⓨ Ⓝ

5. Ⓨ Ⓝ

6. Ⓨ Ⓝ

___ / 6
Total

NAME: _____ **DATE:** _____

DIRECTIONS Read and answer each question.

1. Ⓨ Ⓝ

1. Circle the words that need capital letters.

I heard the song "friends forever" in the movie *girls' day out*.

2. Ⓨ Ⓝ

2. Add an apostrophe to the sentence.

Chloes backyard has the best tree house I have ever seen!

3. Ⓨ Ⓝ

4. Ⓨ Ⓝ

3. Rewrite the sentence using the correct pronoun.

Sasha's mother was not happy about the squirrels in his garden.

5. Ⓨ Ⓝ

_____

6. Ⓨ Ⓝ

_____

___ / 6
Total

4. Write the sentence in past tense.

The astronomer will watch the meteor shower in the sky.

_____

_____

5. Circle the verbs in the sentence.

The seamstress hopes to make a new quilt by next month.

6. Circle the word that is spelled correctly.

city   sitty   sity

NAME: _____ DATE: _____

DIRECTIONS Read and answer each question.

1. Circle the words that need capital letters.

The title of the video game is *speed demon*.

2. Rewrite *the pet belongs to Sofia* using an apostrophe.

_____

3. Write the sentence in present tense.

I will go to the library every day during summer vacation.

_____

_____

4. Write two adjectives to complete the sentence.

The _____, _____ rainbow
in the sky was a beautiful sight to see.

5. Circle the verbs in the sentence.

The nurse held the newborn baby
while the mom got dressed.

6. Circle the word that is spelled correctly.

siy   siye   sigh

NAME: _____ **DATE:** _____

DIRECTIONS Read and answer each question.

1. Add quotation marks and a comma to the sentence.

1. Ⓨ Ⓝ

That is the new student in our class   remarked Cara.

2. Ⓨ Ⓝ

2. Add apostrophes to the sentence.

3. Ⓨ Ⓝ

Marias ears felt funny on the airplane, and Mothers ears also did not feel normal.

4. Ⓨ Ⓝ

3. Circle the adjectives in the sentence.

5. Ⓨ Ⓝ

The pretty flower will go well in the bouquet.

6. Ⓨ Ⓝ

4. Circle the adverb in the sentence.

____ / 6
Total

José's mom divided the cookie evenly in two pieces.

5. Write the correct verb to complete the sentence.

Can the airplane still _____ even if there is a storm outside?
(fly, flew, flown)

6. Add an *-ing* ending to the base word *swim*. Write the word on the line.

_____

NAME: _____ **DATE:** _____

DIRECTIONS Read and answer each question.

1. Circle the words that need capital letters.

....

The book I wish I could read next is <u>the baseball hero</u>.

....

1. Ⓨ Ⓝ

2. Ⓨ Ⓝ

2. Add an apostrophe to the sentence.

....

The babysitters mistake was saying yes to a snowball fight.

....

3. Ⓨ Ⓝ

3. Write the correct pronoun to complete the sentence.

....

Anna wanted to make _____ tree house out of wood.
                                      (her, his, their)

....

4. Ⓨ Ⓝ

5. Ⓨ Ⓝ

4. Circle the adjectives in the sentence.

....

The warm muffin was on the menu at
our special restaurant.

....

6. Ⓨ Ⓝ

___ / 6
Total

5. Write a sentence using the plural noun *children*.

_____

_____

6. Circle the word that is spelled correctly.

....

allmost   allmowst   almost

....

NAME: _____ **DATE:** _____

DIRECTIONS Read and answer each question.

1. Add apostrophes to the sentence.

....

Rosies soccer uniform was mixed up with her sisters uniform.

....

2. Use an apostrophe to write *the food that belongs to Hank* in another way.

_____

3. Circle the adjective in the sentence.

....

Nina's new bike was fun to ride yesterday.

....

4. Many plural nouns end in *-s* or *-es*. Circle the noun that does **not** follow this rule.

....

ring   mouse   hat

....

5. Circle the adverbs in the sentence.

....

Kara lovingly hugged her sister before she quickly boarded the plane.

....

6. Add an *-ed* ending to the base word *drag*.
Write the word on the line.

_____

NAME: _____ **DATE:** _____

DIRECTIONS Read and answer each question.

1. Add a comma to the sentence.

I hope that we can go on vacation to New Orleans Louisiana.

1. Ⓨ Ⓝ

2. Ⓨ Ⓝ

2. Add a comma to the following address.

90 Torrey Road

Vancouver WA 98330

3. Ⓨ Ⓝ

4. Ⓨ Ⓝ

3. Write the correct verb to complete the sentence.

Will the bell _____ before we have a chance to play kickball?
(ring, rang, rung)

5. Ⓨ Ⓝ

6. Ⓨ Ⓝ

4. Write two adjectives that would make sense in the sentence.

Aiden and Parker watched the _____,
_____ game and decided not to play.

___ / 6
Total

5. Circle the verb in the sentence.

Lily jumped in the puddle on the rainy day.

6. Add a -tion ending to the base word *celebrate*. Write the word on the line.

_____

NAME: _____ **DATE:** _____

DIRECTIONS Read and answer each question.

1. (Y) (N)

1. Add a comma to the following address.

778 Hanover Street
Honolulu HI 78944

2. (Y) (N)

2. Use an apostrophe to write *the computer belonging to Pablo* in another way.

3. (Y) (N)

_____

4. (Y) (N)

3. Write the correct verb to complete the sentence.

5. (Y) (N)

I am earning money for my school by _____ laps in a special walk-a-thon event. (walks, walking, walk)

6. (Y) (N)

4. Write two adjectives to complete the sentence.

___ / 6
Total

The _____, _____ hot chocolate was the perfect treat on a cold day.

5. Circle the pronoun in the sentence.

Grace left her flute at home on the day of band practice.

6. Add an *-ing* ending to the base word *spot*. Write the word on the line.

_____

NAME: _____ **DATE:** _____

DIRECTIONS Read and answer each question.

1. Circle the words in the sentence that need capital letters.

Who knows the words to the song "summertime blues"?

2. Add apostrophes to the sentence.

The teachers students were quiet while they listened to Mrs. Walters directions.

3. Write the correct verb to complete the sentence.

Yesterday's snowfall _____ we get to have a day off from school. (mean, means, meaning)

4. Circle the adverb in the sentence.

Good friends almost always play happily together.

5. Write the correct pronoun to complete the sentence.

Steven wanted to bring _____ video game to school but that was against the rules. (his, her, their)

6. Circle the word that is spelled correctly.

soap   sope   soep

NAME: _____ **DATE:** _____

DIRECTIONS Read and answer each question.

1. Y N

1. Circle the words in the sentence that need capital letters.

Mason and I watched the movie *family time* together.

2. Y N

2. Rewrite the sentence using an apostrophe.

3. Y N

The sister of Maria wanted to go to school with her.

4. Y N

_____

_____

5. Y N

3. Write a sentence using the word *kindness*.

_____

6. Y N

_____

___ / 6
Total

4. Circle the adjectives in the sentence.

The curious baby wanted to crawl to reach the loud, blinking toy.

5. Circle the pronoun in the sentence.

Zack was not interested in reading, so he did not check out a library book.

6. Add an *-ing* ending to the base word *rot*. Write the word on the line.

_____

NAME: _____ DATE: _____

DIRECTIONS Read and answer each question.

1. Circle the words in the sentence that need capital letters.

The video game I want for my birthday is called *digging up the ruins*.

1. Ⓨ Ⓝ

2. Ⓨ Ⓝ

2. Use an apostrophe to write *the leg of Samantha* in another way.

_____

3. Ⓨ Ⓝ

3. Write the correct adjective to complete the sentence.

The giraffe at the zoo was the _____ animal I had ever seen.
(tall, taller, tallest)

4. Ⓨ Ⓝ

5. Ⓨ Ⓝ

4. Rewrite the sentence in past tense.

I see the customer pay for the groceries at the store.

_____

_____

6. Ⓨ Ⓝ

___ / 6
Total

5. Circle the adverbs in the sentence.

The rain fell quietly while I slept peacefully in my bed.

6. Circle the word that is spelled correctly.

planely   plainly   plainley

NAME: _____ DATE: _____

Read and answer each question.

SCORE

1. Ⓨ Ⓝ

2. Ⓨ Ⓝ

3. Ⓨ Ⓝ

4. Ⓨ Ⓝ

5. Ⓨ Ⓝ

6. Ⓨ Ⓝ

___ / 6
Total

1. Write *the computer belonging to Fernando* in another way.

_____

2. Add a comma to the following address.

11 Jackson Blvd.
Oakland UT 65710

3. Combine the sentences. Include the word *but*.

My backpack was in my locker. My homework was still missing.

_____

_____

4. Circle the pronoun in the sentence.

Aunt Shirley always invites the family over to her house for dinner.

5. Circle the word that represents future tense.

The car will speed through the tunnel while driving on the highway.

6. Add an *-ing* ending to the base word *hope*. Write the word on the line.

_____

NAME: _____ **DATE:** _____

DIRECTIONS Read and answer each question.

1. Add a comma to the sentence.

Sunit had to move with her family to Orlando Florida.

1. Ⓨ Ⓝ

2. Use an apostrophe to write *the cape of a hero* in another way.

_____

2. Ⓨ Ⓝ

3. Ⓨ Ⓝ

3. Write the correct adjective to complete the sentence.

The rock band played the _____ music I have
ever heard.   (loud, louder, loudest)

4. Ⓨ Ⓝ

5. Ⓨ Ⓝ

4. Write two adverbs that could be used in the sentence.

Our family's pet cat always naps _____ and
_____ in the sun.

6. Ⓨ Ⓝ

___ / 6
Total

5. Write a sentence using the word *misery*.

_____

_____

6. Circle the word that is spelled correctly.

mainely   manely   mainly

NAME: _____ **DATE:** _____

DIRECTIONS Read and answer each question.

SCORE

1. (Y)(N)

1. Circle the words that need capital letters.

....

My grandparents traveled to our home from phoenix, arizona.

....

2. (Y)(N)

2. Add a comma to the following address.

....

88 Easter Street

Xenia IL 88900

....

3. (Y)(N)

3. Circle the transition word in the sentence.

....

I got out of bed, though I wish I were still in bed.

....

4. (Y)(N)

4. Write a sentence using an adverb. Circle the adverb.

_____

_____

5. (Y)(N)

5. Write the plural noun to complete the sentence.

....

The _____ were not able to hear the
　　　　　(child)

teacher's directions.

....

6. (Y)(N)

6. Circle the word that is spelled correctly.

....

cuple　　　　　　　couple　　　　　　　coupel

....

___ / 6
Total

NAME: _____ DATE: _____

DIRECTIONS Read and answer each question.

1. Circle the words that need capital letters.

My family loves to go on vacation to san francisco, california.

2. Add a comma to the address.

54 Hawthorne Street
Carson NV 88900

3. Combine the sentences. Include the word *so*.

The school bus was late to pick us up. We were late to class.

_____

_____

4. Circle the adjectives in the sentence.

Nina cuddled with her fluffy bear to calm her on a stormy night.

5. Circle the past tense verbs in the sentence.

Alfredo ate half of the pizza and had an upset stomach afterward.

6. Add an *-ing* ending to the base word *nap*. Write the word on the line.

_____

1. Ⓨ Ⓝ

2. Ⓨ Ⓝ

3. Ⓨ Ⓝ

4. Ⓨ Ⓝ

5. Ⓨ Ⓝ

6. Ⓨ Ⓝ

___ / 6
Total

NAME: _____   **DATE:** _____

DIRECTIONS   Read and answer each question.

1. Circle the words that need capital letters.

1. Ⓨ Ⓝ

> The post office delivers to newberg, washington, and across the border at hillsborough, oregon.

2. Ⓨ Ⓝ

2. Use an apostrophe to write *the coat that belongs to Lily* in another way.

3. Ⓨ Ⓝ

_____

3. Write a sentence using the word *education.*

4. Ⓨ Ⓝ

_____

5. Ⓨ Ⓝ

_____

4. Write the correct adjective to complete the sentence.

6. Ⓨ Ⓝ

Amanda found a dollar on the ground, so she felt _____

(lucky, luckier, luckiest)

___ / 6
Total

than her brother and sister who did not see the money.

5. Circle the adverb in the sentence.

The bicycle zoomed by quickly as it sped down the hill.

6. Circle the word that is spelled correctly.

scent   sentt   secnt

NAME: _____ **DATE:** _____

DIRECTIONS Read and answer each question.

1. Circle the words that need capital letters.

1. Ⓨ Ⓝ

"I know all of the words to the song, 'that pretty little rainbow,'" bragged Julie.

2. Ⓨ Ⓝ

2. Add an apostrophe to the sentence.

Jacks baseball team won the championship, and they all received trophies!

3. Ⓨ Ⓝ

3. Write the correct verb to complete the sentence.

4. Ⓨ Ⓝ

Rick wanted to _____ the new book he had just
(reading, reads, read)

5. Ⓨ Ⓝ

checked out from the library.

6. Ⓨ Ⓝ

4. Circle the proper noun in the sentence.

___ / 6

Total

My swim coach, Lucy, was not able to come to practice because her daughter was sick.

5. Circle the pronouns in the sentence.

Violet said, "Can you please take care of our puppy while we are on vacation?"

6. Add a -*tion* ending to the base word *create*. Write the word on the line.

_____

NAME: _____ DATE: _____

DIRECTIONS Read and answer each question.

1. (Y) (N)

1. Add quotation marks to the sentence.

Who is going to help me collect homework? the teacher asked.

2. (Y) (N)

2. Use an apostrophe to write *the tools belonging to the scientist* in another way.

_____

3. (Y) (N)

3. Circle the transition word in the sentence.

I had to go to piano lessons after school, although I really wanted to go home instead.

4. (Y) (N)

4. Write two adjectives that make sense in the sentence.

The _____, _____ sunrise was beautiful to watch.

5. (Y) (N)

5. Add a verb to complete the sentence.

The bus _____ around the city.

6. (Y) (N)

6. Circle the word that is spelled correctly.

weigh   wiegh   waygh

___ / 6
Total

NAME: _____ DATE: _____

| DIRECTIONS | Read and answer each question. |

1. Add quotation marks to the sentence.

1. Ⓨ Ⓝ

....

Why am I always the last one to get picked for the team? Liam complained.

2. Ⓨ Ⓝ

....

2. Add apostrophes to the sentence.

3. Ⓨ Ⓝ

....

Alexs birthday invitation list includes Oscars sister.

....

4. Ⓨ Ⓝ

3. Write a sentence using the word *recess.*

_____

5. Ⓨ Ⓝ

_____

6. Ⓨ Ⓝ

4. Write two adverbs that complete the sentence.

....

___ / 6

The cat moved _____ and _____
across the lawn.

Total

....

5. Write the plural form of *man* to complete the sentence.

....

A group of _____ worked together to push the car.

....

6. Add an *-ion* ending to the base word *immigrate*. Write it on the line.

_____

NAME: _____ **DATE:** _____

DIRECTIONS Read and answer each question.

1. Write the name of a city and state. Use a comma correctly.

_____

1. Ⓨ Ⓝ

2. Circle another way to write *the pet of a friend*.

2. Ⓨ Ⓝ

a friend's pet   a friends pet   a friend,s pet

3. Ⓨ Ⓝ

3. Combine the sentences. Include the words *as long as*.

4. Ⓨ Ⓝ

The baby will go to bed. She has her bottle first.

5. Ⓨ Ⓝ

_____

_____

6. Ⓨ Ⓝ

4. Write an adjective to complete the sentence.

___ / 6
Total

The _____ bird was easy for the birdwatcher to spot in the tree.

5. Circle the plural noun in the sentence.

The city is a great place to visit museums.

6. Circle the word that is spelled correctly.

chare   chaer   chair

NAME: _____ **DATE:** _____

DIRECTIONS Read and answer each question.

1. Add commas to the sentence.

Destiny and Brittany wanted to visit Rome Italy together.

2. What is another way to write *the hair on Mom*?

Mom's hair　　　Moms hair　　　Moms' hair

3. Circle the nouns in the sentence.

The girl walked to her house on a sunny day.

4. Write an adverb to complete the sentence.

The jet flew _____ across the sky above our house.

5. Circle the adverb in the sentence.

The door in the old house creaked loudly as I opened it.

6. Circle the word that is spelled correctly.

where

wher

whear

1. Ⓨ Ⓝ

2. Ⓨ Ⓝ

3. Ⓨ Ⓝ

4. Ⓨ Ⓝ

5. Ⓨ Ⓝ

6. Ⓨ Ⓝ

___ / 6
Total

NAME: _____ DATE: _____

DIRECTIONS Read and answer each question.

SCORE

1. Ⓨ Ⓝ

1. Circle the words in the sentence that need capital letters.

At the roller rink, they played the song "stop causing trouble."

2. Ⓨ Ⓝ

2. Write *the ice cream belonging to Tracy* in another way.

3. Ⓨ Ⓝ

_____

3. Circle the plural noun in the sentence.

4. Ⓨ Ⓝ

When I was lost at the park, the women who worked there helped me find my mom.

5. Ⓨ Ⓝ

4. Write the correct verb to complete the sentence.

6. Ⓨ Ⓝ

Rafael asked, "What can I _____ at the mall today?"
(spend, spent, spending)

___ / 6
Total

5. Combine the sentences. Include the word *but*.

We should see the orca whales in the ocean. We may have an unlucky day.

_____

_____

6. Add an *-ing* ending to the base word *tap*. Write the word on the line.

_____

 #51168—180 Days of Language

NAME: _____ **DATE:** _____

DIRECTIONS Read and answer each question.

1. Add a comma to the following address.

46577 Parkview Place

Seattle WA 59004

2. Use an apostrophe to write *the toy car belonging to Oliver* in another way.

_____

3. Write the correct verb to complete the sentence.

On Easter morning, Lucy hopes to _____ the most eggs.
(find, found, finds)

4. Write the correct noun to complete the sentence.

The student sat at a new _____ for the first
time yesterday.   (desk, chair, floor)

5. Circle the adverb in the sentence.

Birds may be communicating secretly with their songs.

6. Circle the word that is spelled correctly.

cornur   corner   korner

1. Ⓨ Ⓝ

2. Ⓨ Ⓝ

3. Ⓨ Ⓝ

4. Ⓨ Ⓝ

5. Ⓨ Ⓝ

6. Ⓨ Ⓝ

___ / 6
Total

NAME: _____ **DATE:** _____

DIRECTIONS Read and answer each question.

1. Y N

1. Add a comma to the following address.

490 Whitehaven Road
Dallas TX 40399

2. Y N

2. Add apostrophes to the sentence.

3. Y N

Sarahs game was rained out
and rescheduled for tomorrow.

4. Y N

3. Circle the conjunction in the sentence.

I don't like to wake up early, and I don't like to go to bed early.

5. Y N

6. Y N

4. Write the correct verb to complete the sentence.

____ / 6
Total

Jesse _____ under the bed during a game of Hide and Seek.
(hid, hiding, hided)

5. Complete the sentence with the plural form of *child*.

The _____ love going to summer camp each year.

6. Circle the word that is spelled correctly.

befor   befour   before

NAME: _____ **DATE:** _____

DIRECTIONS Read and answer each question.

1. Circle the words that need capital letters.

I think that the poem titled "the wind calls my name" is very beautiful.

2. Add an apostrophe to the sentence.

Martins favorite hobby is collecting stamps and coins.

3. Write the correct verb to complete the sentence.

The class wanted to _____ a game of kickball at recess.
(play, plays, playing)

4. Circle the adjectives in the sentence.

The yellow sunflower began to poke out of the damp soil.

5. Write the plural noun to complete the sentence.

The _____ read books to relax on their vacation.
(woman)

6. Add an *-ing* ending to the base word *bake*. Write the word on the line.

_____

1. (Y)(N)

2. (Y)(N)

3. (Y)(N)

4. (Y)(N)

5. (Y)(N)

6. (Y)(N)

___ / 6
Total

NAME: _____ DATE: _____

DIRECTIONS Read and answer each question.

1. Y N

1. Circle the words that need capital letters.

....

Kassie is trying to learn how to play "when the sun comes up" on the piano.

2. Y N

....

2. Use an apostrophe to write *the candy that belongs to Ted* in another way.

3. Y N

_____

4. Y N

3. Write a sentence using an adverb that describes how you moved at recess time.

5. Y N

_____

_____

6. Y N

4. Write the correct verb to complete the sentence.

....

___ / 6
Total

Whom do I _____ if I need help in an emergency?
(call, calls, calling)

....

5. Circle the adverb in the sentence.

....

We have to leave soon to get a table at the busy restaurant.

....

6. Add a *-ness* ending to the base word *worthy*. Write it on the line.

_____

NAME: _____ **DATE:** _____

DIRECTIONS Read and answer each question.

1. Add a comma to the sentence.

There are many desert wildflowers near Phoenix Arizona.

1. Ⓨ Ⓝ

2. Add an apostrophe to the sentence.

Jacksons skateboard was brand new and a lot of fun to ride.

2. Ⓨ Ⓝ

3. Ⓨ Ⓝ

3. Write a sentence using the word *determination.*

_____

_____

4. Ⓨ Ⓝ

5. Ⓨ Ⓝ

4. Write the nouns below in the plural form.

6. Ⓨ Ⓝ

child _____ woman _____

man _____ tooth _____

___ / 6
Total

5. Write the correct verb to complete the sentence.

The polar bear _____ up from his long nap.
(wake, woke, woken)

6. Add a *-tion* ending to the base word *compete.* Write it on the line.

_____

NAME: _____ **DATE:** _____

| DIRECTIONS | Read and answer each question. |

1. Y N

2. Y N

3. Y N

4. Y N

5. Y N

6. Y N

___ / 6
Total

1. Add a comma to the following address.

5550 Arrowhead Way

Lake Tahoe CA 89772

2. Write *the water that belongs to Ava* in another way.

_____

3. Write the correct verb to complete the sentence.

Lisa said, "I hope we do not _____ our soccer game
tomorrow."   (lose, lost, losing)

4. Write an adjective to complete the sentence.

This _____ vacation is so much fun.

5. Write a sentence using an adjective to describe an object in
your bedroom.

_____

_____

6. Circle the word that is spelled correctly.

latly   lattely   lately

NAME: _____ DATE: _____

DIRECTIONS Read and answer each question.

1. Write an address. Be sure to include a comma.

_____

_____

1. Ⓨ Ⓝ

2. Ⓨ Ⓝ

2. Add apostrophes to the sentence.

Harpers dog was not getting along with Mayas dog.

3. Ⓨ Ⓝ

3. Write a sentence using the word *quest.*

_____

_____

4. Ⓨ Ⓝ

5. Ⓨ Ⓝ

6. Ⓨ Ⓝ

4. Circle the pronouns in the sentence.

She is nearly six years old because her birthday is next week.

___ / 6
Total

5. Complete the sentence with the plural form of *man.*

The _____ played football at the park all morning.

6. Circle the word that is spelled correctly.

suddenly   suddenley   suddinly

NAME: _____ DATE: _____

DIRECTIONS Read and answer each question.

1. Y N

2. Y N

3. Y N

4. Y N

5. Y N

6. Y N

___ / 6
Total

1. Circle the words in the sentence that need capital letters.

It is difficult to play the song "stomping along" on the piano.

2. Circle another way to write *the owner of a store*.

the store's owner   the stores' owner   the stores owner

3. Rewrite the sentence in past tense.

The hummingbird flaps its wings very quickly.

_____

_____

4. Circle the adjectives in the sentence.

The blue bird sat on a thick branch during the hot day.

5. Circle the plural noun in the sentence.

My dentist really wants me to take better care of my teeth.

6. Circle the word that is spelled correctly.

sadniss   sadnes   sadness

NAME: _____ **DATE:** _____

DIRECTIONS Read and answer each question.

1. Circle the words in the sentence that need capital letters.

1. Ⓨ Ⓝ

How many syllables are in the haiku poem titled "the beautiful forest"?

2. Ⓨ Ⓝ

2. Add quotation marks and a comma to the sentence.

3. Ⓨ Ⓝ

I prefer pepperoni pizza over cheese pizza   replied Claire.

4. Ⓨ Ⓝ

3. Which adjective makes the most sense in the sentence?

5. Ⓨ Ⓝ

Santiago's _____ shoes were getting to be way too tight.   (old, scary, confusing)

6. Ⓨ Ⓝ

4. Write the correct verb to complete the sentence.

___ / 6
Total

I promised my mom I would _____ in the car while she ran inside.   (stay, stays, staying)

5. Circle the adverb in the sentence.

Santiago shyly asked his teacher for a snack at recess time.

6. Add an *-er* ending to the base word *thin*. Write it on the line.

_____

NAME: _____ DATE: _____

DIRECTIONS Read and answer each question.

1. Circle the words that need capital letters.

"Hey Mom, I just noticed that the video game titled *baseball championship* is on sale," said Rodrigo.

2. Add commas to the sentence.

The moving van was traveling from Houston Texas to Miami Florida.

3. Circle the possessive nouns in the sentence.

Jacob's football was missing, so Walter's mom looked for it in the garage.

4. Circle the verbs in the sentence.

Her wrist was hurt after she fell from the swingset.

5. Rewrite the sentence in future tense.

Our class picnic took place on Friday afternoon.

_____

_____

5. Circle the word that is spelled correctly.

kinder   kynder   kindr

NAME: _____ DATE: _____

DIRECTIONS Read and answer each question.

1. Add a comma to the following address.

6855 Hawthorne Road
Portland OR 90222

2. Use an apostrophe to write *the report card belonging to Jayden* in another way.

_____

3. Circle the conjunction in the sentence.

I want a bike for my birthday, and I hope that my bike is purple.

4. Write two adjectives to complete the sentence.

The _____, _____ waves crashed loudly at the beach.

5. Write the correct verb to complete the sentence.

Parker _____ a secret to his sister.
      (telling, telled, told)

6. Add an *-est* ending to the base word *safe*. Write it on the line.

_____

1. Ⓨ Ⓝ

2. Ⓨ Ⓝ

3. Ⓨ Ⓝ

4. Ⓨ Ⓝ

5. Ⓨ Ⓝ

6. Ⓨ Ⓝ

___ / 6
Total

NAME: _____ **DATE:** _____

DIRECTIONS Read and answer each question.

1. Add quotation marks and a comma to the sentence.

1. Y N

This homework is taking too long complained Nate.

2. Y N

2. Add apostrophes to the sentence.

3. Y N

Don't you want to go to Milos party to celebrate
Milos birthday?

4. Y N

3. Write the correct adjective to complete the sentence.

5. Y N

Abigail felt that the math test was _____ than the
spelling test.   (hard, harder, hardest)

6. Y N

4. Circle the adverb in the sentence.

___ / 6
Total

I slowly opened the door because I did not know who was knocking.

5. Rewrite the sentence in past tense.

Jack and Carol walk to the swimming pool together.

_____

_____

6. Circle the word that is spelled correctly.

shipmint   shipmeant   shipment

 #51168—180 Days of Language

NAME: _____ **DATE:** _____

DIRECTIONS Read and answer each question.

1. Use an apostrophe to write *the door for my classroom* in another way.

_____

1. Ⓨ Ⓝ

2. Add quotation marks and a comma to the sentence.

That construction work woke me up too early complained Dad.

2. Ⓨ Ⓝ

3. Ⓨ Ⓝ

3. Write a sentence using the noun *peace.*

_____

_____

4. Ⓨ Ⓝ

5. Ⓨ Ⓝ

4. Circle the adjectives in the sentence.

The happy man smiled at his young child at the amusement park.

6. Ⓨ Ⓝ

___ / 6
Total

5. Write the plural noun to complete the sentence.

Liam's _____ were hurting after stepping on glass.
(foot)

6. Circle the word that is spelled correctly.

nearer   neerer   nearur

NAME: _____ **DATE:** _____

DIRECTIONS Read and answer each question.

1. Add a comma to the following address.

650 Jackson Street

Templeton NC 69440

2. Add quotation marks and a comma to the sentence.

I think that Grandpa laughs the most at his own jokes Chris said.

3. Rewrite the sentence in future tense.

The leash on the dog was too tight, so June loosened it.

_____

_____

4. Many plural nouns end in -s or -es. Circle the noun that does **not** follow this rule.

flower   glass   tooth

5. Circle the adverbs in the sentence.

Mom calmly told me to come inside even after I refused repeatedly.

6. Add an -er ending to the base word *funny*. Write the word on the line.

_____

NAME: _____ **DATE:** _____

| DIRECTIONS | Read and answer each question. |

1. Add commas to the sentence.

There are many old buildings in Rome Italy and Berlin Germany.

1. Ⓨ Ⓝ

2. Add an apostrophe to the sentence.

The dogs fleas made him scratch.

2. Ⓨ Ⓝ

3. Ⓨ Ⓝ

3. Rewrite the sentence in past tense.

The whale comes up from the water and pokes its nose in the air.

_____

_____

4. Ⓨ Ⓝ

5. Ⓨ Ⓝ

6. Ⓨ Ⓝ

4. Write a sentence using the noun *patience.*

_____

_____

___ / 6
Total

5. Circle the adjectives in the sentence.

Our family rule is that the person closest to the door goes out first.

6. Circle the word that is spelled correctly.

preeheat   preaheat   preheat

NAME: _____ DATE: _____

DIRECTIONS Read and answer each question.

1. (Y)(N)

1. Add quotation marks and a comma to the sentence.

I am not sure if I want to go to the slumber party   Ellen said.

2. (Y)(N)

2. Use an apostrophe to write *the edge of the table* in another way.

_____

3. (Y)(N)

3. Circle the adverb in sentence A below.

4. (Y)(N)

4. Underline the pronoun in sentence A below.

A   He wanted to walk quietly down the hall at night.

5. (Y)(N)

5. Circle the adjectives in the sentence.

___/6
Total

The lifelong friends argued loudly about the soccer game.

6. (Y)(N)

6. Add an *-est* ending to the base word *easy*. Write it on the line.

_____

NAME: _____ DATE: _____

DIRECTIONS Read and answer each question.

1. Create an address. Be sure to include a comma.

_____

_____

1. Ⓨ Ⓝ

2. Add apostrophes to the sentence.

Harry isn't afraid of Peters dog, but he is afraid of Peters brother.

2. Ⓨ Ⓝ

3. Ⓨ Ⓝ

3. Circle the adjectives in the sentence.

I watched the race to see the fast runners.

4. Ⓨ Ⓝ

5. Ⓨ Ⓝ

4. Circle the adverb in the sentence.

The lock fit tightly on the door.

6. Ⓨ Ⓝ

___ / 6
Total

5. Rewrite the sentence in future tense.

No one came to the soccer practice because of the rain.

_____

_____

6. Circle the word that is spelled correctly.

unluckie   unluky   unlucky

NAME: _____ **DATE:** _____

DIRECTIONS Read and answer each question.

1. Y N

1. Add a comma to the following address.

4430 Northwest 50th Street

New York NY 89220

2. Y N

2. Use an apostrophe to write *the buttons on the phone* in another way.

3. Y N

_____

3. Write a sentence with an adverb. Circle the adverb.

4. Y N

_____

_____

5. Y N

6. Y N

4. Circle the adjectives in the sentence.

The shiny penny was easy to spot on the sandy beach.

___ / 6
Total

5. Write the plural noun to complete the sentence.

The _____ boarded the bus after the women got on.
     (man)

6. Add an *-est* ending to the base word *small*. Write the word on the line.

_____

NAME: _____ **DATE:** _____

DIRECTIONS Read and answer each question.

1. Add quotation marks and a comma to the sentence.

Mrs. Sanchez remarked   I am proud of how hard you all worked today.

1. Ⓨ Ⓝ

2. Circle another way to write *the dance recital starring Dana*.

Danas dance recital   Dana's dance recital   Danas' dance recital

2. Ⓨ Ⓝ

3. Ⓨ Ⓝ

3. Circle the past tense verbs in the sentence.

Nola's dog ran on the beach and played in the waves.

4. Ⓨ Ⓝ

5. Ⓨ Ⓝ

4. Many plural nouns end in -*s* or -*es*. Circle the noun that does **not** follow this rule.

lip   hair   tooth

6. Ⓨ Ⓝ

___ / 6
Total

5. Circle the adverbs in the sentence.

We watched quietly as the dolphin dove deeply in the water.

6. Circle the word that is spelled correctly.

untye   unti   untie

NAME: _____ **DATE:** _____

SCORE

| DIRECTIONS | Read and answer each question. |

1. Ⓨ Ⓝ

1. Circle another way to write *the backpack belonging to Gus*.

Gus's backpack   Guss backpack   Guses backpack

2. Ⓨ Ⓝ

2. Add quotation marks and a comma to the sentence.

My dad yelled   Be careful riding your bike on the street!

3. Ⓨ Ⓝ

3. Circle the adjectives in sentence A below.

4. Ⓨ Ⓝ

4. Underline the pronoun in sentence A below.

Ⓐ   The small, white puppy was our favorite one in the litter.

5. Ⓨ Ⓝ

5. Write the correct adjective to complete the sentence.

6. Ⓨ Ⓝ

My face was the _____ in the class after I got my sunburn.
(red, redder, reddest)

____ / 6
Total

6. Add an *-er* ending to the base word *silly*. Write the word on the line.

_____

NAME: _____ **DATE:** _____

SCORE

DIRECTIONS   Read and answer each question.

1. Write a city and state that you would like to visit. Be sure to include a comma.

_____

1. Ⓨ Ⓝ

2. Use an apostrophe to write *the apple belonging to Wade* in another way.

_____

2. Ⓨ Ⓝ

3. Ⓨ Ⓝ

3. Write a sentence with a pronoun. Circle the pronoun.

_____

_____

4. Ⓨ Ⓝ

5. Ⓨ Ⓝ

4. Write two adjectives that could be used in the sentence.

The _____ and _____ gift from Uncle Steve at my birthday party was my favorite.

6. Ⓨ Ⓝ

___ / 6
Total

5. Write the correct adjective to complete the sentence.

It was _____ to celebrate my birthday with my
          (wonderful, awful, sad)

family and friends.

6. Add a *-ness* ending to the base word *quiet*. Write the word on the line.

_____

NAME: _____ **DATE:** _____

DIRECTIONS Read and answer each question.

1. Add quotation marks and a comma to the sentence.

The lifeguard shouted   It's break time, so you need to get out of the pool!

2. Add an apostrophe to the sentence.

A giraffes neck helps it to reach food in tall trees.

3. Circle the adverb in the sentence.

Climbing that mountain was extremely difficult.

4. Write the correct verb to complete the sentence.

Who _____ at the red table for math?
       (sitting, sat, sitted)

5. Write the plural noun of *woman* to fit in the blank.

The _____ ate lunch in the lunchroom and then returned to their desks.

6. Circle the word that is spelled correctly.

tuff   tough   tugh

NAME: _____ DATE: _____

DIRECTIONS Read and answer each question.

1. Circle the words in the sentence that need capital letters.

Is that a piano that plays in the background of the song "move your body"?

1. Ⓨ Ⓝ

2. Ⓨ Ⓝ

2. Use an apostrophe to write *the bike belonging to Jack* in another way.

_____

3. Ⓨ Ⓝ

3. Write the correct adjective to complete the sentence.

4. Ⓨ Ⓝ

Violet is not the _____ student in her class.
                    (tall, taller, tallest)

5. Ⓨ Ⓝ

6. Ⓨ Ⓝ

4. Circle the nouns in the sentence.

Diego has been asking for warm soup for his birthday dinner.

___ / 6
Total

5. Rewrite the sentence in the past tense.

The loose tooth could fall out soon.

_____

_____

6. Write a word that has the same *-est* spelling pattern as in *fastest*.

_____

NAME: _____ **DATE:** _____

DIRECTIONS Read and answer each question.

1. Circle the words in the sentence that need capital letters.

I loved listening to my teacher read poetry aloud, especially the poem titled "waves crashing silently."

2. Add an apostrophe to the sentence.

The hot water burned Kerrys hand.

3. Rewrite the sentence in past tense.

Rita's toy is so real looking that people are surprised it is a doll.

_____

_____

4. Write the nouns below in the plural form.

child _____ mouse _____

5. Circle the adverb in the sentence.

Nora anxiously waited for the school bus.

6. Write a word that has the same -ful spelling pattern as in *hopeful*.

_____

NAME: _____ DATE: _____

DIRECTIONS Read and answer each question.

1. Add a comma to the following address.

440 Hancock Way

Oklahoma City OK 60550

1. Ⓨ Ⓝ

2. Ⓨ Ⓝ

2. Add quotation marks and a comma to the sentence.

We can help endangered species in many ways
the scientist explained.

3. Ⓨ Ⓝ

3. Circle the adjectives in sentence A below.

4. Ⓨ Ⓝ

5. Ⓨ Ⓝ

4. Underline the pronoun in sentence A below.

Ⓐ   Aiden is a big fan of sports, and he loves to collect trading cards.

6. Ⓨ Ⓝ

___ / 6
Total

5. Write an adjective to complete the sentence.

I chose the _____ shirt to wear to school today.

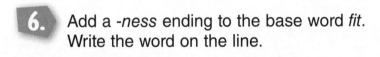

6. Add a -ness ending to the base word *fit*.
Write the word on the line.

_____

NAME: _____ DATE: _____

SCORE

DIRECTIONS Read and answer each question.

1. Add quotation marks and a comma to the sentence.

1. Ⓨ Ⓝ

Look who came to school wearing a new skirt remarked Candace.

2. Ⓨ Ⓝ

2. Use an apostrophe to write *the wrinkles on the hippopotamus* in another way.

3. Ⓨ Ⓝ

_____

4. Ⓨ Ⓝ

3. Write the correct adverb to complete the sentence.

5. Ⓨ Ⓝ

Lois _____ helps put her baby sister in the car.
(often, more often)

6. Ⓨ Ⓝ

4. Write two adverbs that could be used in the sentence.

___ / 6
Total

Kira's baby sister crawled _____ and _____ on the floor.

5. Write the correct verb to complete the sentence.

The school photographer _____ our class picture this morning. (took, take, taken)

6. Add a *-ment* ending to the base word *pay*. Write the word on the line.

_____

NAME: _____ DATE: _____

| DIRECTIONS | Read and answer each question. |

1. Add commas to the sentence.

Where is Milwaukee Wisconsin on the map?

2. Add apostrophes to the sentence.

Shes always safe on her sisters bike, but she is not used to riding her brothers scooter.

3. Write the correct adjective to complete the sentence.

The 1945 penny was the _____ one in my entire collection.　　(shiny, shinier, shiniest)

4. Circle the adverb in the sentence.

It is nice to know that my mom will greet me happily every day after school.

5. Write the plural form of *child* to complete the sentence.

The group of _____ sat still during class.

6. Add an *-able* ending to the base word *value*. Write the word on the line.

_____

1. Ⓨ Ⓝ

2. Ⓨ Ⓝ

3. Ⓨ Ⓝ

4. Ⓨ Ⓝ

5. Ⓨ Ⓝ

6. Ⓨ Ⓝ

___ / 6
Total

NAME: _____ DATE: _____

SCORE

1. Ⓨ Ⓝ

2. Ⓨ Ⓝ

3. Ⓨ Ⓝ

4. Ⓨ Ⓝ

5. Ⓨ Ⓝ

6. Ⓨ Ⓝ

___ / 6
Total

DIRECTIONS Read and answer each question.

1. Circle the words in the sentence that need capital letters.

Should we sing "love you forever" as a trio or as a duet?

2. Use an apostrophe to write *the dress of Olivia* in another way.

_____

3. Write a sentence using the word *memory*.

_____

_____

4. Circle the adjectives in the sentence.

Yummy cupcakes are delicious treats.

5. Write the plural noun to complete the sentence.

The big white _____ lived on the farm.
(goose)

6. Write a word that has the same *-ight* spelling pattern as in *delight*.

_____

NAME: _____ DATE: _____

DIRECTIONS Read and answer each question.

1. Add a comma to the following address.

> 3009 Hartford Road
>
> Chicago IL 75884

2. Write *the bike belonging to Sophia* in another way.

_____

3. Write two adjectives to describe a classmate.

_____   _____

4. Many plural nouns end in *-s* or *-es*. Circle the noun that does **not** follow this rule.

deer   friend   team

5. Circle the adverb in the sentence.

> My chore list says that I must walk my dog daily.

6. Circle the word that is spelled correctly.

rereed   rearead   reread

NAME: _____ DATE: _____

DIRECTIONS Read and answer each question.

1. Write a sentence about a song you like. Be sure to use capital letters.

_____

_____

1. Ⓨ Ⓝ

2. Ⓨ Ⓝ

2. Add quotation marks to the sentence.

3. Ⓨ Ⓝ

Who should be the line leader today? Paul asked his teacher.

4. Ⓨ Ⓝ

3. Write the correct adjective to complete the sentence.

5. Ⓨ Ⓝ

The smoke was so _____ that we could not see through it.   (black, blackly, blackest)

6. Ⓨ Ⓝ

___ / 6
Total

4. Circle the adjectives in sentence A below.

5. Underline the adverbs in sentence A below.

Ⓐ The young child danced excitedly while the rock band played loudly.

6. Circle the word that is spelled correctly.

tight

tiete

tite

NAME: _____ **DATE:** _____

DIRECTIONS   Read and answer each question.

1. Write a sentence about where you were born. Be sure to include a comma.

_____

_____

1. Ⓨ Ⓝ

2. Ⓨ Ⓝ

2. Add quotation marks to the sentence.

How much longer until lunch? Sam complained.

3. Ⓨ Ⓝ

3. Write the correct adjective to complete the sentence.

I think there are spring days that feel _____ than winter days.   (cold, colder, coldest)

4. Ⓨ Ⓝ

5. Ⓨ Ⓝ

6. Ⓨ Ⓝ

4. Write two adverbs to complete the sentence.

The large ship sailed _____ and _____ on the open sea.

___ / 6
Total

5. Circle the **first** verb in the sentence.

I wrote the directions to the store so that my mom could find her way.

6. Write a word that has the same *re-* spelling pattern as in *reheat*.

_____

NAME: _____ **DATE:** _____

DIRECTIONS Read and answer each question.

1. Circle the types of words that are always capitalized.

song titles   compound words   adjectives

2. Add apostrophes to the sentence.

The ships captain cant stop working while sailing because it is the captains job.

3. Write a sentence using the word *laughter.*

_____

_____

4. Circle the adjectives in sentence A below.

5. Underline the adverb in sentence A below.

A The long worm slithered slowly through the wet ground.

6. Write a word that has the same *pre-* spelling pattern as in *pretest.*

_____

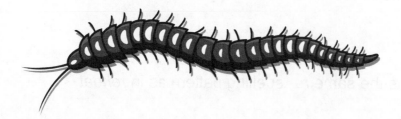

 #51168—180 Days of Language

NAME: _____ DATE: _____

DIRECTIONS Read and answer each question.

1. Circle the words that need capital letters.

I think I know all of the words to the song "uncle john's farm."

1. Ⓨ Ⓝ

2. Use an apostrophe to write *the drum set belonging to Erik* in another way.

_____

2. Ⓨ Ⓝ

3. Ⓨ Ⓝ

3. Write the correct adjective to complete the sentence.

The cheetah is one of the _____ animals in the world.
(fast, faster, fastest)

4. Ⓨ Ⓝ

5. Ⓨ Ⓝ

4. Circle the nouns in sentence A below.

6. Ⓨ Ⓝ

5. Underline the adverbs in sentence A below.

Ⓐ I quickly ate the muffin and then sneakily tried some pancakes.

___ / 6
Total

6. Write a word that has the same *-est* spelling pattern in *easiest*.

_____

NAME: _____ **DATE:** _____

DIRECTIONS Read and answer each question.

1. Add quotation marks to the sentence.

1. (Y)(N)

I am very excited for the holiday parade today! exclaimed Rosa.

2. (Y)(N)

2. Write *the water bottle belonging to José* in another way.

3. (Y)(N)

_____

3. Write the correct verb to complete the sentence.

4. (Y)(N)

My parents _____ some rest so they went
(needs, needed, needing)

5. (Y)(N)

on a vacation and left us here with my grandparents.

6. (Y)(N)

4. Many plural nouns end in *-s* or *-es*. Circle the noun that does **not** follow this rule.

___ / 6
Total

boat   goose   drink

5. Circle the adverbs in the sentence.

Marco quietly slipped out of his bed and quickly got dressed.

6. Write a word that has the same *-ment* spelling pattern as in *apartment*.

_____

NAME: _____ **DATE:** _____

DIRECTIONS Read and answer each question.

1. Write the name of a state capital and its state. Be sure to include a comma.

_____

1. Ⓨ Ⓝ

2. Add apostrophes to the sentence.

Would you like to go to Hanks house or Jesses house after school?

2. Ⓨ Ⓝ

3. Ⓨ Ⓝ

3. Write a sentence using the word *truth.*

_____

_____

4. Ⓨ Ⓝ

5. Ⓨ Ⓝ

4. Circle the adjectives in the sentence.

The grocery store is closer to my house than the basketball courts.

6. Ⓨ Ⓝ

___ / 6
Total

5. Write the correct verb to complete the sentence.

How did you _____ after you got a shot at the doctor's office?   (felt, feel, feelings)

6. Circle the word that is spelled correctly.

funnyer   funnier   funneyer

NAME: _____ DATE: _____

Read and answer each question.

SCORE

1. Ⓨ Ⓝ

2. Ⓨ Ⓝ

3. Ⓨ Ⓝ

4. Ⓨ Ⓝ

5. Ⓨ Ⓝ

6. Ⓨ Ⓝ

___ / 6
Total

1. Add a comma to the following address.

4009 Tellium Lane

Jacksonville FL 89403

2. Use an apostrophe to write *the last chapter of the book* in another way.

_____

3. Write the correct verb to complete the sentence.

"Mom, did you _____ Isaac's present yet?" Steven
asked.   (wrap, wraps, wrapped)

4. Write an adverb to complete the sentence.

The marching band played _____ for the crowd along
the parade route.

5. Circle the adjectives in the sentence.

What do you think is the loudest sound in the entire world?

6. Circle the word that is spelled correctly.

cuter   cyooter   cuteer

NAME: _____ **DATE:** _____

DIRECTIONS Read and answer each question.

SCORE

1. Circle the types of words that are always capitalized.

1. Ⓨ Ⓝ

titles of poems   long words   the last words
                                              in sentences

2. Ⓨ Ⓝ

2. Add apostrophes to sentence A below.

3. Ⓨ Ⓝ

3. Underline the pronoun in sentence A below.

4. Ⓨ Ⓝ

Ⓐ The bears cub wandered off from the pack,
but the cubs mother kept a close eye on him.

5. Ⓨ Ⓝ

4. Circle the adverb in the sentence.

6. Ⓨ Ⓝ

The maple leaf fell quietly from the tree.

___ / 6
Total

5. Write a sentence using the word *energy.*

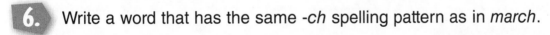

_____

_____

6. Write a word that has the same -*ch* spelling pattern as in *march.*

_____

NAME: _____ **DATE:** _____

SCORE

1. Ⓨ Ⓝ

1. Circle the words that need capital letters.

....

The movie *norm's day out* made me laugh very hard!

....

2. Ⓨ Ⓝ

2. Use an apostrophe to write *the pocket on the backpack* in another way.

_____

3. Ⓨ Ⓝ

3. Write the correct adjective to complete the sentence.

....

4. Ⓨ Ⓝ

I think that the first movie was much _____ than
its sequel.   (funny, funnier, funniest)

5. Ⓨ Ⓝ

....

6. Ⓨ Ⓝ

4. Circle the adjectives in the sentence.

....

The small, blue bird chirped happily from the low branch.

....

___ / 6
Total

5. Write the plural noun to complete the sentence.

....

Lily's _____ were wiggly and about to fall out.
         (tooth)

....

6. Write a word that has the same *kn-* spelling pattern as in *knowing*.

_____

NAME: _____ DATE: _____

DIRECTIONS Read and answer each question.

1. Circle the words that need capital letters.

The movie *earthquake time* is supposed to be very scary.

1. Ⓨ Ⓝ

2. Ⓨ Ⓝ

2. Circle the phrase that shows the correct use of an apostrophe.

Seth's pencil   Seths' pencil   Seths pencil's

3. Ⓨ Ⓝ

3. Rewrite the sentence in the past tense.

Kai's notebook is missing from his backpack.

_____

_____

4. Ⓨ Ⓝ

5. Ⓨ Ⓝ

6. Ⓨ Ⓝ

4. Many plural nouns end in *-s* or *-es*. Circle the noun that does **not** follow this rule.

child   napkin   shoe

___ / 6
Total

5. Circle the adverbs in the sentence.

Nina usually walks to school with Fran, but today she walked happily with Grace.

6. Circle the word that is spelled correctly.

berst   burst   burrst

NAME: _____ DATE: _____

DIRECTIONS Read and answer each question.

1. Circle the words that need capital letters.

My mom bought me the video game *race day*, and it is a fun game.

2. Add quotation marks and a comma to the sentence.

Let's take Buster to the dog park   Brady said.

3. Circle the conjunction in the sentence.

Chloe could order chocolate ice cream at the ice cream parlor, or she could order vanilla.

4. Write the correct verb to complete the sentence.

Yesterday, Ava quickly _____ for the sleepover.
(pack, packs, packed)

5. Circle the adverb in the sentence.

The dog ran quickly to his food bowl.

6. Circle the word that is spelled correctly.

sertain

certen

certain

NAME: _____ **DATE:** _____

DIRECTIONS   Read and answer each question.

1. Circle the item that is always capitalized.

pronouns   adjectives   holidays

2. Use an apostrophe to write *the basket on the bike* in another way.

_____

3. Combine the sentences. Include the word *but.*

Evan had to go to soccer practice. He didn't want to go.

_____

_____

4. Write two adverbs to complete the sentence.

The musician played _____ and _____
while the audience listened.

5. Circle the nouns in the sentence.

Eric and Sam ate sandwiches at lunch.

6. Circle the word that is spelled correctly.

replase   replace   replas

1. Ⓨ Ⓝ

2. Ⓨ Ⓝ

3. Ⓨ Ⓝ

4. Ⓨ Ⓝ

5. Ⓨ Ⓝ

6. Ⓨ Ⓝ

___ / 6
Total

NAME: _____ **DATE:** _____

| DIRECTIONS | Read and answer each question. |

SCORE

1. Ⓨ Ⓝ

2. Ⓨ Ⓝ

3. Ⓨ Ⓝ

4. Ⓨ Ⓝ

5. Ⓨ Ⓝ

6. Ⓨ Ⓝ

___ / 6
Total

1. Circle the words in the sentence that need capital letters.

I love the dog character in the movie *the cat's meow*.

2. Add apostrophes to the sentence.

Carters coach thought that Carters performance could have been better.

3. Write the correct adjective to complete the sentence.

My grandpa said watching my play made him _____.

(happy, happiest)

4. Circle the adverb in the sentence.

The spider moved quickly to get to the web and eat its food.

5. Write the correct verb to complete the sentence.

I can't hear myself think because there _____ too much noise in here.

(is, was, were)

6. Write a word that has the same *un-* spelling pattern as in *unlock*.

_____

NAME: _____ **DATE:** _____

DIRECTIONS Read and answer each question.

1. Add commas to the sentence.

Buffalo New York is where my grandparents live.

2. Use an apostrophe to write *the high school in the city* in another way.

_____

3. Write the correct adjective to complete the sentence.

Picking flowers for my teacher was a _____ thing to do.
(kind, kindest)

4. Circle the adjectives in sentence A below.

5. Underline the adverb in sentence A below.

Ⓐ The yellow school bus traveled safely to the school.

6. Add an *-est* ending to the base word *quiet*. Write the word on the line.

_____

1. Ⓨ Ⓝ

2. Ⓨ Ⓝ

3. Ⓨ Ⓝ

4. Ⓨ Ⓝ

5. Ⓨ Ⓝ

6. Ⓨ Ⓝ

___ / 6
Total

NAME: _____ **DATE:** _____

DIRECTIONS Read and answer each question.

1. (Y)(N)

2. (Y)(N)

3. (Y)(N)

4. (Y)(N)

5. (Y)(N)

6. (Y)(N)

___ / 6
Total

1. Circle the words that need capital letters.

....

Our music teacher helped us write a new song titled "where we are."

....

2. Rewrite the sentence using an apostrophe.

....

The trampoline belonging to my neighbors was so much fun that we jumped all day!

_____

_____

....

3. Write a pronoun to complete the sentence.

....

Peter rushed out the door, but _____ forgot his lunch.

....

4. Many plural nouns end in *-s* or *-es*. Circle the noun that does **not** follow this rule.

....

mouse   broom   root

....

5. Circle the adverb in the sentence.

....

Some teachers rarely sit all day long at school.

....

6. Add an *-est* ending to the base word *thin*. Write the word on the line.

_____

NAME: _____ **DATE:** _____

DIRECTIONS Read and answer each question.

1. Write a phrase a book character says. Be sure to use a comma and quotation marks.

_____

_____

1. Ⓨ Ⓝ

2. Ⓨ Ⓝ

2. Add an apostrophe to the sentence.

It is Franks opinion that the best time to do your homework is after dinner.

3. Ⓨ Ⓝ

4. Ⓨ Ⓝ

3. Circle the nouns in the sentence.

The farmer got on his tractor and prepared to go out to the field.

5. Ⓨ Ⓝ

6. Ⓨ Ⓝ

4. Write the correct verb to complete the sentence.

Monica wondered if she could _____ time on the computer.   (spend, spent, spending)

___ / 6

Total

5. Circle the pronouns in the sentence.

I cook breakfast for myself, so I can eat before school.

6. Circle the word that is spelled correctly.

amownt   amount   amowent

NAME: _____ DATE: _____

SCORE

DIRECTIONS Read and answer each question.

1. Add quotation marks to the sentence.

1. Ⓨ Ⓝ

....

I love to play in the sprinklers on a hot day! Ruby exclaimed.

....

2. Ⓨ Ⓝ

2. Use an apostrophe to write *the label on the peanut butter jar* in another way.

3. Ⓨ Ⓝ

_____

4. Ⓨ Ⓝ

3. Rewrite the sentence using the correct pronoun.

....

Aunt Maria made his famous chili for the barbecue.

5. Ⓨ Ⓝ

_____

6. Ⓨ Ⓝ

_____

....

___ / 6
Total

4. Write two adverbs to complete the sentence.

....

The woman laughed _____ and _____ at the joke.

....

5. Write two adjectives to complete the sentence.

....

One time I was _____, but now I am _____.

....

6. Circle the word that is spelled correctly.

....

mouth   moweth   mowth

....

NAME: _____ **DATE:** _____

DIRECTIONS Read and answer each question.

1. Add quotation marks and a comma to the sentence.

I am not sure why people always take the shortcut to school observed Jack.

2. Add an apostrophe to the sentence.

The babys bottle was empty, so he started to scream.

3. Rewrite the sentence in past tense.

The zoo train goes by the visitors, and everyone hears the whistle.

_____

_____

4. Circle the adverb in the sentence.

The massive python slithered silently across the ground, and no one could hear it.

5. Circle the part of speech *massive* falls under.

noun   adjective   adverb

6. Add an *-est* ending to the base word *cute*. Write the word on the line.

_____

NAME: _____ **DATE:** _____

DIRECTIONS Read and answer each question.

1. Add quotation marks and a comma to the sentence.

I'd like to walk to the river and sit on the rocks   Nina said.

2. Circle another way to write *the bark on the tree.*

the tree bark   the trees' bark   the tree's bark

3. Write the correct verb to complete the sentence.

Dogs _____ not always friendly animals, so be careful.
        (is, our, are)

4. Circle the adjectives in the sentence.

Grandpa likes to sit in the reclining chair in the living room.

5. Write a sentence using the plural noun *women*.

_____

_____

6. Circle the word that is spelled correctly.

hare   haer   hayr

 #51168—180 Days of Language

NAME: _____ DATE: _____

DIRECTIONS Read and answer each question.

1. Add quotation marks and a comma to the sentence.

Wes shouted   I love going to school!

2. Use an apostrophe to write *the tail of the lion* in another way.

_____

3. Write the correct adjective to complete the sentence.

Our puppy was _____ after playing at the beach than
          (tired, more tired, most tired)

going for a long walk.

4. Many plural nouns end in *-s* or *-es*. Circle the noun that does **not** follow this rule.

cup   mouse   phone

5. Circle the adverbs in the sentence.

The sun shone brightly as Felix played happily at the park.

6. Circle the word that is spelled correctly.

erley   urley   early

NAME: _____ DATE: _____

DIRECTIONS Read and answer each question.

1. Add a comma to the following address.

6044 West Grant Blvd.

San Francisco CA 89004

2. Add a noun to complete the sentence.

At the neighbor's house, _____ played in the backyard all day.

3. Circle the conjunction in the sentence.

Jason loves to play with his friends, but recently he hasn't.

4. Rewrite the sentence in past tense.

Oliver plays video games until dinnertime.

_____

_____

5. Circle the verbs in the sentence.

"Please keep your hands to yourself!" scolded Mom.

6. Add an -ing ending to the base word *choose*. Write the word on the line.

_____

#51168—180 Days of Language

NAME: _____ DATE: _____

DIRECTIONS Read and answer each question.

1. Add commas to the sentence.

....

Aunt Vivian is traveling to Cairo Egypt this summer to see the pyramids.

....

2. Use an apostrophe to write *the ears on Pablo* another way.

_____

3. Write the correct adjective to complete the sentence.

....

Hands feel very _____ after roasting marshmallows.
(sticky, stickier, stickiest)

....

4. Write two adjectives that could be used in the sentence.

....

The band's lead singer performed a _____,

_____ song.

....

5. Complete the sentence with a verb.

....

My friends can _____ all by themselves.

....

6. Circle the word that is spelled correctly.

....

morening   morning   moerning

....

1. Ⓨ Ⓝ

2. Ⓨ Ⓝ

3. Ⓨ Ⓝ

4. Ⓨ Ⓝ

5. Ⓨ Ⓝ

6. Ⓨ Ⓝ

___ / 6
Total

NAME: _____ DATE: _____

DIRECTIONS Read and answer each question.

1. Add a comma and quotation marks to the sentence.

1. Ⓨ Ⓝ

I wonder if there will be a goody bag at the birthday party Jessica commented.

2. Ⓨ Ⓝ

2. Write *the computer belonging to the teacher* in another way.

3. Ⓨ Ⓝ

_____

3. Rewrite the sentence in the past tense.

4. Ⓨ Ⓝ

The mother cat sleeps in the sun while the kittens play around her.

5. Ⓨ Ⓝ

_____

6. Ⓨ Ⓝ

_____

_____

___ / 6
Total

4. Circle the past tense form of the word *ride*.

rided   roded   rode

5. Circle the conjunction in the sentence.

Sally can go to the swimming pool, or she can go to the playground.

6. Add an *-ing* ending to the base word *take*. Write the word on the line.

_____

NAME: _____ **DATE:** _____

DIRECTIONS Read and answer each question.

1. Add a comma to the following address.

603 Grainger Blvd.
Alameda CA 89004

1. Ⓨ Ⓝ

2. Ⓨ Ⓝ

2. Write *the ending of the book* in another way.

_____

3. Ⓨ Ⓝ

4. Ⓨ Ⓝ

3. Circle the conjunction in the sentence.

Iris had to finish her homework, but she had soccer practice first.

5. Ⓨ Ⓝ

4. Circle the adjectives in the sentence.

The rude man cut in line, so the angry customers complained to the frustrated employee.

6. Ⓨ Ⓝ

___/ 6
Total

5. Rewrite the sentence in past tense.

Sam and Jack swim in the pool to stay cool.

_____

_____

6. Write another word that has the spelling pattern *-ore*, as in *before*.

_____

NAME: _____ **DATE:** _____

SCORE

1. Ⓨ Ⓝ

2. Ⓨ Ⓝ

3. Ⓨ Ⓝ

4. Ⓨ Ⓝ

5. Ⓨ Ⓝ

6. Ⓨ Ⓝ

____ / 6
Total

1. Circle the words in the sentence that need capital letters.

I am going to ask my mom to buy me the album with the song titled "life goes on."

2. Use an apostrophe to write *the fishing pole belonging to Lance* in another way.

_____

3. Circle the adjectives in the sentence.

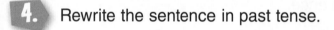

Max is a helpful student.

4. Rewrite the sentence in past tense.

I teach my friend how to play soccer.

_____

_____

5. Circle the adverb in the sentence.

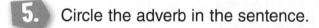

The music played loudly at the game.

6. Add an *-ed* ending to the base word *trip*. Write the word on the line.

_____

NAME: _____ DATE: _____

DIRECTIONS Read and answer each question.

1. Add quotation marks to the sentence.

1. Ⓨ Ⓝ

I wish you two would stop fighting over the video game! Mom pleaded.

2. Ⓨ Ⓝ

2. Add an apostrophe to the sentence.

3. Ⓨ Ⓝ

Teresas teacher was absent on Friday.

4. Ⓨ Ⓝ

3. Write the correct adjective to complete the sentence.

5. Ⓨ Ⓝ

I heard many sounds in the early morning, but the rooster was

much _____ than the train's whistle.
(loud, louder, loudest)

6. Ⓨ Ⓝ

4. Write a sentence using the word *kindness.*

___ / 6
Total

_____

_____

5. Write the correct verb to complete the sentence.

At yesterday's race, the runners _____
themselves at how fast they ran. (surprise, surprising, surprised)

6. Write another word that has the spelling pattern *-ear* as in *wear.*

_____

NAME: _____ **DATE:** _____

DIRECTIONS Read and answer each question.

1. (Y)(N)

2. (Y)(N)

3. (Y)(N)

4. (Y)(N)

5. (Y)(N)

6. (Y)(N)

___ / 6
Total

1. Add quotation marks and a comma to the sentence.

Mr. Winters called out Who is buying lunch today?

2. Use an apostrophe to write the *uniform of the soccer goalie* in another way.

_____

3. Circle the pronouns in the sentence.

Dan likes to ride his skateboard, but today he was not interested.

4. Write an adjective that could be used in the sentence.

The _____ book was hard to put down, so Tim read for hours.

5. Write a sentence using the word *wisdom.*

_____

_____

6. Circle the word that is spelled correctly.

foreget   fourget   forget

NAME: _____ **DATE:** _____

| DIRECTIONS | Read and answer each question. |

1. Write the name of a city and a state. Be sure to include a comma.

_____

1. Ⓨ Ⓝ

2. Write *the bike belonging to Miss Jones* in another way.

_____

2. Ⓨ Ⓝ

3. Ⓨ Ⓝ

3. Write the correct adjective to complete the sentence.

4. Ⓨ Ⓝ

Mrs. Roberts thought that Evan was the _____ kid at the party because he ate the most.   (hungry, hungrier, hungriest)

5. Ⓨ Ⓝ

4. Write a sentence about how you ride a bike using an adverb.

_____

_____

6. Ⓨ Ⓝ

5. Write a sentence about the sky using an adjective.

_____

_____

____ / 6

Total

6. Add an *-ed* ending to the base word *spot*. Write the word on the line.

_____

NAME: _____   **DATE:** _____

SCORE

1. (Y)(N)

2. (Y)(N)

3. (Y)(N)

4. (Y)(N)

5. (Y)(N)

6. (Y)(N)

___ / 6
Total

1. Add a city and state to the following address. Be sure to include correct punctuation.

4009 Harper Road

_____ _____ 49281

2. Add quotation marks to the sentence.

How are we going to celebrate my birthday?
Jessie wondered.

3. Circle the verb in the sentence.

Carter warned his classmates about the challenging test.

4. Circle the adjectives in the sentence.

At night, I sleep on a fluffy pillow.

5. Write a sentence using the plural noun *teeth*.

_____

_____

6. Circle the word that is spelled correctly.

fuir   ferr   fur

NAME: _____ **DATE:** _____

Read and answer each question.

SCORE

1. Add quotation marks to the sentence.

Who was the first person to finish the test? Cal wondered.

1. Ⓨ Ⓝ

2. Use an apostrophe to write *the saxophone belonging to Maria* in another way.

_____

2. Ⓨ Ⓝ

3. Ⓨ Ⓝ

3. Write the correct adjective to complete the sentence.

At the zoo, the monkeys looked like the _____ animals to be stuck in a cage.   (sad, sadder, saddest)

4. Ⓨ Ⓝ

5. Ⓨ Ⓝ

4. Many plural nouns end in *-s* or *-es*. Circle the noun that does **not** follow this rule.

hand   rug   ox

6. Ⓨ Ⓝ

___ / 6
Total

5. Circle the adverb in the sentence.

Tina screamed loudly to get her pet's attention.

6. Circle the word that is spelled correctly.

kurl   cerl   curl

NAME: _____ DATE: _____

DIRECTIONS Read and answer each question.

1. Circle the words in the sentence that need capital letters.

I decided to read my poem titled "summer fun" for the poetry fair.

2. Add a city and state to the address. Be sure to include a comma.

1299 Hoover Street

_____ _____ 57577

3. Circle the adjectives in the sentence.

John is quiet for his teacher.

4. Rewrite the sentence in past tense.

The artist makes the painting in her art studio.

_____

_____

5. Write a sentence using the word *gossip.*

_____

_____

6. Write a word that has the same *cir-* spelling pattern as in *circus.*

_____

NAME: _____ **DATE:** _____

DIRECTIONS Read and answer each question.

1. Circle the words that need capital letters.

I made up a dance to the song that is titled "jump, jump, jump."

1. Ⓨ Ⓝ

2. Add quotation marks to the sentence.

Olive, can you come to my birthday party? Kate asked.

2. Ⓨ Ⓝ

3. Ⓨ Ⓝ

3. Circle the pronoun in the sentence.

Kara and her mom walked to school together.

4. Ⓨ Ⓝ

5. Ⓨ Ⓝ

4. Write two adjectives that could be used in the sentence.

Our _____ and _____ pet chewed Dad's shoes again.

6. Ⓨ Ⓝ

___ / 6
Total

5. Rewrite the sentence in future tense.

The puppies cuddled up to their mother.

_____

_____

6. Circle the word that is spelled correctly.

touch   toutch   tutch

NAME: _____ **DATE:** _____

DIRECTIONS Read and answer each question.

1. Circle the words that need capital letters.

1. Ⓨ Ⓝ

The ballet class performed to the song "slow symphony."

2. Ⓨ Ⓝ

2. Add quotation marks to the sentence.

3. Ⓨ Ⓝ

The nurse said, I am sorry, but I have to give you a shot.

4. Ⓨ Ⓝ

3. Write the correct verb to complete the sentence.

5. Ⓨ Ⓝ

The watch was _____ to me by my grandmother for my birthday. (give, gave, given)

6. Ⓨ Ⓝ

4. Write the correct adverb that makes sense in the sentence.

___ / 6
Total

It was a beautiful summer day, and the sisters swam _____ together.
(happily, curiously, heavily)

5. Write the correct verb to complete the sentence.

The sisters _____ until they took a break from the game. (argued, argue)

6. Circle the word that is spelled correctly.

owr   our   ouer

NAME: _____ **DATE:** _____

DIRECTIONS Read and answer each question.

1. Circle the words in the sentence that need capital letters.

I have to write a book report on a book titled <u>in mother's memory</u>.

2. Add quotation marks to the sentence.

I hope you have a really great birthday, Mom said to me this morning.

3. Circle the conjunction in the sentence.

I would like to go home, but I will stay longer.

4. Circle the adjectives in the sentence.

The small bird flapped its wings.

5. Rewrite the sentence in the past tense.

I tear the paper to make a collage for my art project.

_____

_____

6. Write another word that has the spelling pattern -ook as in shook.

_____

1. Ⓨ Ⓝ

2. Ⓨ Ⓝ

3. Ⓨ Ⓝ

4. Ⓨ Ⓝ

5. Ⓨ Ⓝ

6. Ⓨ Ⓝ

___ / 6
Total

NAME: _____   **DATE:** _____

SCORE

1. (Y)(N)

2. (Y)(N)

3. (Y)(N)

4. (Y)(N)

5. (Y)(N)

6. (Y)(N)

___ / 6
Total

DIRECTIONS   Read and answer each question.

1. Circle the words in the sentence that need capital letters.

Our class published a book that is titled <u>facts about our solar system</u>.

2. Use an apostrophe to write *the collar on the dog* in another way.

_____

3. Circle the pronouns in the sentence.

Spirit Day was today, and we were supposed to dress up like our favorite book characters.

4. Rewrite the sentence in past tense.

I wake up first thing in the morning when the sun comes up.

_____

_____

5. Circle the adverb in the sentence.

The phone rang loudly.

6. Write another word that has the spelling pattern -*ash* as in *splash*.

_____

NAME: _____ DATE: _____

DIRECTIONS Read and answer each question.

1. Add a comma to the following address.

430 North Main Street
Honolulu HI 58998

1. Ⓨ Ⓝ

2. Ⓨ Ⓝ

2. Add an apostrophe to the sentence.

The students bullying was not tolerated at school.

3. Ⓨ Ⓝ

3. Circle the adjectives in the sentence.

The blue and red flowers are blooming.

4. Ⓨ Ⓝ

5. Ⓨ Ⓝ

6. Ⓨ Ⓝ

4. Circle the conjunction in the sentence.

The baby bird wants to leave the nest, yet the mama bird wants to take care of him.

___ / 6
Total

5. Write the correct verb to complete the sentence.

My friend and I _____ hungry, so we helped ourselves to a snack. (is, was, were)

6. Write another word that has the spelling pattern -*tch* as in *scratch*.

_____

NAME: _____ **DATE:** _____

| **DIRECTIONS** | Read and answer each question. |

1. Circle the words that need capital letters.

1. Ⓨ Ⓝ

Kevin wanted to play *football mania* or *truck-race warrior*.

2. Ⓨ Ⓝ

2. Use an apostrophe to write the *saddle of a horse* in another way.

3. Ⓨ Ⓝ

_____

3. Write the correct adverb to complete the sentence.

4. Ⓨ Ⓝ

After I was sent to the principal's office, my mom was the

5. Ⓨ Ⓝ

_____ I have ever seen her.

(upset, more upset, most upset)

6. Ⓨ Ⓝ

4. Write an adjective to complete the sentence.

___ / 6
Total

Playing in the pool is fun on a _____ day.

5. Write the correct verb to complete the sentence.

Helmets _____ required before we could go on a
bike ride.   (were, was, is)

6. Circle the word that is spelled correctly.

circus   sircus   cirkus

NAME: _____ **DATE:** _____

DIRECTIONS Read and answer each question.

1. Write the name of a city and state. Be sure to include a comma.

_____

1. Ⓨ Ⓝ

2. Add quotation marks to the sentence.

I really don't like having ants in my room! shouted Leah.

2. Ⓨ Ⓝ

3. Ⓨ Ⓝ

3. Use a pronoun to write a sentence about your morning. Circle the pronoun.

_____

_____

4. Ⓨ Ⓝ

4. Use an adverb to write a sentence about what you did at recess.

_____

_____

5. Ⓨ Ⓝ

6. Ⓨ Ⓝ

___ / 6
Total

5. Use an adjective to write about what a school day is like.

_____

_____

6. Add an -ed ending to the base word *stop*. Write the word on the line.

_____

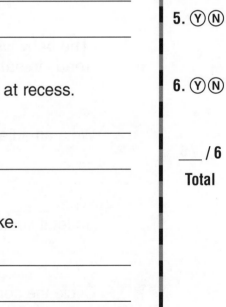

NAME: _____ **DATE:** _____

DIRECTIONS Read and answer each question.

SCORE

1. (Y)(N)

2. (Y)(N)

3. (Y)(N)

4. (Y)(N)

5. (Y)(N)

6. (Y)(N)

___ / 6
Total

1. Add quotation marks to the sentence.

....

I can't believe it is almost spring break! Johnny exclaimed.

....

2. Add apostrophes to the sentence.

....

Henrys mom and Alanas dad were both chaperones on the field trip.

....

3. Write the correct verb to complete the sentence.

....

The baby will only _____ when he is hungry and ready to eat.   (cry, cried, cries)

....

4. Write an adjective to complete the sentence.

....

The _____ soup was too hot to eat, so we had to let it cool.

....

5. Circle the correct past tense form of the word *write*.

....

writing   wrote   write

....

6. Circle the word that is spelled correctly.

....

careful   carefull   cairful

....

NAME: _____ **DATE:** _____

DIRECTIONS Read and answer each question.

1. Circle the words that need capital letters.

1. Ⓨ Ⓝ

I read the book <u>sophie's adventure</u> at the library.

2. Ⓨ Ⓝ

2. Use an apostrophe to write *a game belonging to a friend* in another way.

_____

3. Ⓨ Ⓝ

3. Circle the pronoun in the sentence.

4. Ⓨ Ⓝ

Parker thought he heard something outside the tent.

5. Ⓨ Ⓝ

4. Write an adverb to complete the sentence.

6. Ⓨ Ⓝ

Logan skateboarded _____, and then he got hurt and had to take a break.

___ / 6
Total

5. Circle the adjectives in the sentence.

Wes has red and brown hair.

6. Circle the word that is spelled correctly.

joiful   joyful   joyfull

NAME: _____ DATE: _____

DIRECTIONS Read and answer each question.

1. Add quotation marks to the sentence.

Should we go to the library or the park first? Mom asked.

2. Add an apostrophe to the sentence.

Jacks group is still getting its work done.

3. Circle the pronouns in the sentence.

I am very excited to see you.

4. Write the correct adverb to complete the sentence.

I can stay up _____ on the weekends than I can on school nights.   (late, later, latest)

5. Write the correct verb to complete the sentence.

After a summer of swim lessons, Claire could _____ in the deep end by herself.   (swam, swim, swimming)

6. Add an *-er* ending to the base word *quiet*. Write the word on the line.

_____

NAME: _____ **DATE:** _____

DIRECTIONS Read and answer each question.

1. Circle the item that is always capitalized.

pronouns   brand names   words in letters

2. Write *the mother of your friend* in another way.

_____

3. Rewrite the sentence in past tense.

Hank wants to go to the lake and fish all day.

_____

_____

4. Write an adverb to complete the sentence.

At the park, Max yelled _____ so that his friends could hear him.

5. Circle the past tense form of the word *make*.

maked   maken   made

6. Circle the word that is spelled correctly.

rinkle   wrinkle   wrinckle

NAME: _____ **DATE:** _____

| DIRECTIONS | Read and answer each question. |

1. Ⓨ Ⓝ

2. Ⓨ Ⓝ

3. Ⓨ Ⓝ

4. Ⓨ Ⓝ

5. Ⓨ Ⓝ

6. Ⓨ Ⓝ

___ / 6
Total

1. Circle the item that is always capitalized.

adjectives   titles   food names

2. Add apostrophes to the sentence.

Gus wasnt sure that the pools heater was turned on because the waters temperature was so low.

3. Write the correct adjective to complete the sentence.

Monday was the _____ day we have had all season.
(warm, warmer, warmest)

4. Circle the adverb in the sentence.

Sophie ran out on the soccer field quickly.

5. Write the past tense form of the word *pay* to complete the sentence.

The boss _____ his workers on the first of the month.

6. Add an *-en* ending to the base word *dark*. Write the word on the line.

_____

NAME: _____ **DATE:** _____

DIRECTIONS Read and answer each question.

1. Circle the words that need capital letters.

I watched my friends play the video game titled *public arena*.

2. Add quotation marks to the sentence.

Who should be on our team for kickball? Lisa wondered.

3. Rewrite the sentence in past tense.

Air pollution is a huge problem, and companies are part of the problem.

_____

_____

4. Circle the adjectives in the sentence.

The brown bear walked along the icy river, looking for fresh salmon to eat.

5. Circle the plural nouns in the sentence.

The cars were involved in an accident, and the drivers had to talk.

6. Circle the word that is spelled correctly.

major   madejer   mayjor

NAME: _____ **DATE:** _____

DIRECTIONS Read and answer each question.

1. Write two cities in your country using correct capitalization.

City One: _____

City Two: _____

2. Use an apostrophe to write *the cafeteria at our school* in another way.

_____

3. Write the correct verb to complete the sentence.

Our choir will _____ for a large audience of 200 people.
(sing, sang, sung)

4. Many plural nouns end in *-s* or *-es*. Circle the noun that does **not** follow this rule.

fire   flame   moose

5. Circle the adverbs in the sentence.

Who can ride a bike quickly and safely?

6. Circle the word that is spelled correctly.

wunder

oneder

wonder

NAME: _____ **DATE:** _____

DIRECTIONS   Read and answer each question.

1. Write the title of your favorite song using correct capitalization.

_____

1. Ⓨ Ⓝ

2. Add apostrophes to the sentence.

The teachers plan for the day was to get the students desks cleaned out.

2. Ⓨ Ⓝ

3. Ⓨ Ⓝ

3. Rewrite the sentence in present tense.

The teaching staff decided to honor the best students.

_____

_____

4. Ⓨ Ⓝ

5. Ⓨ Ⓝ

6. Ⓨ Ⓝ

4. Write the correct adverb to complete the sentence.

Who do you think is the _____ athlete in the world?   (famous, most famous)

___ / 6
Total

5. Write the correct verb to complete the sentence.

You are not _____ to have friends over today.
      (allow, allowed, allowing)

6. Add the *pre-* prefix to the base word *view*. Write the word on the line.

_____

NAME: _____ DATE: _____

DIRECTIONS Read and answer each question.

1. Add a comma to the following address.

276 West Road

Concord NH 29855

2. Add apostrophes to the sentence.

Averys bird would not stop chirping,
so Averys mother had to cover the cage.

3. Circle the nouns in the sentence.

Scientists watched the whales to study their patterns.

4. Write two adjectives that describe homework.

_____   _____

5. Write the correct verb to complete the sentence.

School _____ in September, and I'm excited about it.
(begun, begins)

6. Circle the word that is spelled correctly.

poet   poit   poeet

NAME: _____ DATE: _____

DIRECTIONS Read and answer each question.

1. Add commas to the sentence.

Mexico City Mexico is a capital city that I would like to visit.

2. Add apostrophes to the sentence.

The dog park is closed because the parks gates are broken and the dogs safety is at risk.

3. Rewrite the sentence in future tense.

The bald eagle soared over the blue river.

_____

_____

4. Write two adjectives that describe cafeteria food.

_____   _____

5. Circle the past tense verb in the sentence.

For centuries, the predators roamed the land in search of food.

6. Write another word that has the spelling pattern *-le* as in *bottle*.

_____

NAME: _____ **DATE:** _____

DIRECTIONS Read and answer each question.

1. Write a sentence about a special city and country you would like to visit. Be sure to use correct punctuation.

_____

_____

2. Add apostrophes to the sentence.

Hannahs sweater is very special because her mothers sister made it for her.

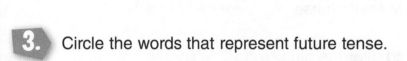

3. Circle the words that represent future tense.

The rain will stop, so we can finally go out for recess!

4. Write a noun to complete the sentence.

The bright _____ attracted all the bees, so we steered clear.

5. Circle the past tense form of the word *catch*.

catched   catchy   caught

6. Add the *un-* prefix to the base word *lock*. Write the word on the line.

_____

NAME: _____ **DATE:** _____

DIRECTIONS Read and answer each question.

1. Circle the words in the sentence that need capital letters.

The poem "party time" was written by a famous poet.

1. Ⓨ Ⓝ

2. Ⓨ Ⓝ

2. Write two objects that belong to your classmates. Be sure to include apostrophes.

_____

_____

3. Ⓨ Ⓝ

4. Ⓨ Ⓝ

3. Write the correct adverb to complete the sentence.

Can you get your homework done _____ so that we
can go out to dinner?   (soon, soonest)

5. Ⓨ Ⓝ

6. Ⓨ Ⓝ

4. Write an adverb to complete the sentence.

The police car sped _____ down the road, so the
passenger cars pulled over.

____ / 6
Total

5. Circle the adjectives in the sentence.

The funny teacher told harmless jokes during the lesson.

6. Circle the word that is spelled correctly.

toff   tuff   tough

NAME: _____ **DATE:** _____

SCORE

1. Ⓨ Ⓝ

2. Ⓨ Ⓝ

3. Ⓨ Ⓝ

4. Ⓨ Ⓝ

5. Ⓨ Ⓝ

6. Ⓨ Ⓝ

___ / 6
Total

DIRECTIONS Read and answer each question.

1. Write two book titles. Be sure to use capital letters.

_____

_____

2. Write two examples of things that belong to your family members. Be sure to include apostrophes.

_____

_____

3. Circle the adjectives in the sentence.

Jackson ate yummy cheese pizza and crisp carrots for dinner.

4. Write the correct verb to complete the sentence.

The baby calf _____ his mother and cuddled up to her.   (find, found, finding)

5. Write the correct pronoun to complete the sentence.

The ant is able to carry huge, heavy objects by _____.
(herself, itself, themselves)

6. Circle the word that is spelled correctly.

happines   happiness   happinness

NAME: _____ DATE: _____

DIRECTIONS Read and answer each question.

1. Circle the item that will always be capitalized.

1. Ⓨ Ⓝ

| words in quotation marks | titles of books | nouns |

2. Ⓨ Ⓝ

2. Circle another way to write *the pencil that belongs to Olivia*.

3. Ⓨ Ⓝ

Olivia's pencil   Olivias' pencil   Olivias pencil

4. Ⓨ Ⓝ

3. Rewrite the sentence in past tense.

Sylvia feeds her cat and sets the table at night.

5. Ⓨ Ⓝ

_____

_____

6. Ⓨ Ⓝ

4. Write two adverbs to complete the sentence.

___ / 6
Total

The clown juggled the balls _____ and

_____ during the performance.

5. Circle the past tense form of the word *pay*.

payed   payd   paid

6. Add a *-less* ending to the base word *hope*. Write the word on the line.

_____

NAME: _____ DATE: _____

DIRECTIONS Read and answer each question.

1. Add a comma to the following address.

8920 Applegate Street
Houston TX 90221

2. Add an apostrophe to the sentence.

The seals whiskers were moving
as he looked for food.

3. Circle the conjunction in the sentence.

I can go to the swimming pool, but I have to clean my room first.

4. Write the correct adverb that makes sense in the sentence.

The students _____ put away their backpacks to start
their day.   (clearly, quickly, equally)

5. Write the past tense form of the verb *mean* to complete the sentence.

Yesterday, I _____ to take my lunch box home, but
I forgot.

6. Add an *-ed* ending to the base word *hope*. Write the word on the line.

_____

NAME: _____ DATE: _____

DIRECTIONS Read and answer each question.

1. Circle the words that need capital letters.

....

Ted wrote a poem and titled it "days go on and on."

....

2. Use an apostrophe to write *the engine of the airplane* in another way.

_____

3. Choose which word best fits in the blank.

....

The baby's skin was much _____ than my own skin.
(soft, softer, softest)

....

4. Many plural nouns end in *-s* or *-es*. Which noun does **not** follow this rule?

....

sheep   bear   lion

....

5. Circle the adverbs in the sentence.

....

Our kitten playfully swatted the ball of yarn while we watched happily.

....

6. Write another word that has the spelling pattern *-eer* as in *cheer*.

_____

NAME: _____ **DATE:** _____

SCORE

DIRECTIONS Read and answer each question.

1. Ⓨ Ⓝ

2. Ⓨ Ⓝ

3. Ⓨ Ⓝ

4. Ⓨ Ⓝ

5. Ⓨ Ⓝ

6. Ⓨ Ⓝ

___ / 6
Total

1. Circle the words in the sentence that need capital letters.

Every holiday, we always sing the same silly song, "those were the days."

2. Add quotation marks to the sentence.

Frank commented, I wonder what will be on our math test today.

3. Circle the past tense verb in the sentence.

Who ate the rest of the birthday cake?

4. Circle the adjectives in the sentence.

The beautiful shrub bloomed and is now covered with bright, red flowers.

5. Write the plural noun to complete the sentence.

Would the _____ be able to check my ticket before I enter?
(man)

6. Circle the word that is spelled correctly.

insted   innsted   instead

NAME: _____ **DATE:** _____

DIRECTIONS Read and answer each question.

1. Add quotation marks to the sentence.

One of these days, I want to learn how to play guitar, Donny said.

2. Add apostrophes to the sentence.

"I hope that Pauls toy is not broken because of Jakes mistake," John commented.

3. Circle the adverb in the sentence.

The storm moved quickly and caused a lot of damage.

4. Rewrite the sentence using the correct pronoun.

Finn's dad was a great soccer coach, and all the players respected her.

_____

_____

5. Circle the adjectives in the sentence.

This was the rainiest week ever recorded in July.

6. Circle the word that is spelled correctly.

brekfast   breakfast   breakfist

1. Ⓨ Ⓝ

2. Ⓨ Ⓝ

3. Ⓨ Ⓝ

4. Ⓨ Ⓝ

5. Ⓨ Ⓝ

6. Ⓨ Ⓝ

___ / 6
Total

NAME: _____ **DATE:** _____

SCORE

DIRECTIONS Read and answer each question.

1. Ⓨ Ⓝ

1. Circle the item that will always be capitalized.

song titles   dialogue words   descriptive words

2. Ⓨ Ⓝ

2. Use an apostrophe to write *roof on the house* in another way.

3. Ⓨ Ⓝ

_____

3. Write the correct verb to complete the sentence.

4. Ⓨ Ⓝ

In the nature show, my favorite part was watching the

antelopes _____.

5. Ⓨ Ⓝ   (run, ran)

4. Write two adjectives to describe your last holiday celebration.

6. Ⓨ Ⓝ

_____   _____

___ / 6
Total

5. Circle the pronouns in the sentence.

When camping, I don't like to sleep in
my tent alone.

6. Add a *-ful* ending to the base word *care*.
Write the word on the line.

_____

NAME: _____ **DATE:** _____

Read and answer each question.

1. Circle the words in the sentence that need capital letters.

The audience wanted to hear the song titled "tender kisses" at the concert.

2. Add an apostrophe to the sentence.

Kevins aunt and uncle are the nicest people in the world.

3. Rewrite the sentence using the correct pronoun.

Maya's mom was going to drive himself to work.

_____

_____

4. Circle the adverb in the sentence.

We cheerfully visited Grandpa at the hospital.

5. Circle the adjectives in the sentence.

The small tortoise was faster than the big hare.

6. Circle the word that is spelled correctly.

sweatr   sweater   sweatur

1. Ⓨ Ⓝ

2. Ⓨ Ⓝ

3. Ⓨ Ⓝ

4. Ⓨ Ⓝ

5. Ⓨ Ⓝ

6. Ⓨ Ⓝ

___ / 6
Total

NAME: _____ DATE: _____

DIRECTIONS Read and answer each question.

SCORE

1. Ⓨ Ⓝ

2. Ⓨ Ⓝ

3. Ⓨ Ⓝ

4. Ⓨ Ⓝ

5. Ⓨ Ⓝ

6. Ⓨ Ⓝ

___ / 6
Total

1. Add a comma to the following address.

759 Walnut Blvd.
Tampa Bay FL 58990

2. Add quotation marks to the sentence.

Who do you think would have taken my bike?
Patrick wondered.

3. Circle the nouns in the sentence.

The librarian told Drew that his book was still missing.

4. Write a sentence using the word *comfort*.

_____

_____

5. What is the past tense form of the word *write*?

wrate   wrote   writing

6. Circle the word that is spelled correctly.

flood   flud   fluud

NAME: _____ DATE: _____

DIRECTIONS Read and answer each question.

1. Circle the words in the sentence that need capital letters.

1. Ⓨ Ⓝ

....

"Mom, will you sing 'hello my baby' to me like you used to?"
Ella asked.

2. Ⓨ Ⓝ

....

2. Add apostrophes to the sentence.

3. Ⓨ Ⓝ

....

Hals music teacher wished that
Hals practice time would increase.

3. Write the correct pronoun to complete the sentence.

4. Ⓨ Ⓝ

....

Zia wanted to have _____ friends over for a sleepover.
(her, him, she)

5. Ⓨ Ⓝ

6. Ⓨ Ⓝ

....

4. Write an adjective to complete the sentence.

___ / 6
Total

....

I noticed the _____ bike right away
when I got to the park.

....

5. Write the correct adjective to complete the sentence.

....

My parents gave me a _____ computer for my birthday.
(new, an, the)

....

6. Write another word that has the spelling pattern *qui-* as in *quick*.

_____

NAME: _____ **DATE:** _____

DIRECTIONS Read and answer each question.

1. Ⓨ Ⓝ

2. Ⓨ Ⓝ

3. Ⓨ Ⓝ

4. Ⓨ Ⓝ

5. Ⓨ Ⓝ

6. Ⓨ Ⓝ

___ / 6
Total

1. Add a comma to the following address.

5894 Harvard Place

New Haven UT 84770

2. Add an apostrophe to the sentence.

The principals secretary was in charge of calling parents.

3. Write the correct adverb to complete the sentence.

Ryder's report card showed that he worked _____
all year.   (hard, hardest)

4. Circle the pronoun in the sentence.

Heather loved to bake, so she decided to
have a bake sale.

5. Write the correct verb to complete the sentence.

I can't _____ until my family goes on vacation!
          (wait, waited, waiting)

6. Write another word that has the spelling pattern *squ-* as in *squeeze*.

_____

NAME: _____ **DATE:** _____

DIRECTIONS Read and answer each question.

1. Circle another way to write *the robot belonging to Noah*.

Noahs robot's   Noahs' robot   Noah's robot

2. Write *the time machine belonging to the mad scientist* in another way.

_____

3. Write an adverb to complete the sentence.

Rodrigo and Ian play the video game _____.

4. Circle the conjunction in the sentence.

I like to watch scary movies, and I like to watch cartoons, too.

5. What is the past tense form of the word *sting*?

stang   stung   stinged

6. Circle the word that is spelled correctly.

balieve

believe

beleev

1. Ⓨ Ⓝ

2. Ⓨ Ⓝ

3. Ⓨ Ⓝ

4. Ⓨ Ⓝ

5. Ⓨ Ⓝ

6. Ⓨ Ⓝ

___ / 6
Total

NAME: _____ DATE: _____

DIRECTIONS Read and answer each question.

SCORE

1. Ⓨ Ⓝ

1. Add quotation marks to the sentence.

Mom, when will I be able to walk to school by myself?
Oscar wondered.

2. Ⓨ Ⓝ

3. Ⓨ Ⓝ

2. Add apostrophes to the sentence.

Carters baseball team was able to beat Lukes baseball team.

4. Ⓨ Ⓝ

3. Circle the nouns in the sentence.

The boat came to shore and headed toward the dock.

5. Ⓨ Ⓝ

6. Ⓨ Ⓝ

4. Write the correct adverb to complete the sentence.

___ / 6
Total

Olivia cleaned her dirty room _____ so that her
friends could come over.   (quickly, sadly, evenly)

5. Circle the noun in the sentence that you cannot experience with one of
your five senses.

Grandma felt pride when she watched her granddaughter get
a medal.

6. Circle the word that is spelled correctly.

neether   niether   neither

NAME: _____ **DATE:** _____

DIRECTIONS Read and answer each question.

1. Circle the words in the sentence that need capital letters.

Grandpa always sings "long, long ago" to his grandchildren.

1. Ⓨ Ⓝ

2. Ⓨ Ⓝ

2. Write a sentence of dialogue. Be sure to include quotation marks and a comma.

_____

_____

3. Ⓨ Ⓝ

4. Ⓨ Ⓝ

3. Write the correct pronoun to complete the sentence.

Pablo loves to play hockey on the ice with _____ brother.
(their, his, her)

5. Ⓨ Ⓝ

6. Ⓨ Ⓝ

4. Circle the adjectives in the sentence.

The brave surfer stayed in the cold ocean water.

___ / 6
Total

5. Circle the plural noun in the sentence.

My dentist told me that if I make sure to floss my teeth, I would keep them clean.

6. Circle the word that is spelled correctly.

clothez   clothes   klothes

NAME: _____ **DATE:** _____

DIRECTIONS Read and answer each question.

1. Circle the words in the sentence that need capital letters.

If you translate the song title from Spanish, it is called "oh, promise me."

2. Use an apostrophe to write *the gown on the princess* in another way.

_____

3. Write the correct pronoun to complete the sentence.

My dad washed _____ family car and asked the kids to help him. (their, our, her)

4. Many plural nouns end in *-s* or *-es*. Circle the noun that does **not** follow this rule.

sea   child   water

5. Circle the adverb in the sentence.

The puppy playfully nipped at the hard bone.

6. Circle the word that is spelled correctly.

moyst

moist

moiset

NAME: _____ **DATE:** _____

DIRECTIONS Read and answer each question.

1. Write a sentence of dialogue that a magician might say to an audience. Be sure to include a comma and quotation marks.

_____

_____

_____

2. Add an apostrophe to the sentence.

We went to my grandmas house for a barbecue.

3. Write a pronoun to complete the sentence.

While the king gave directions to the kingdom, the people listened

closely to _____.

4. Write the correct verb to complete the sentence.

Last month, choir _____ to compete in the state
competition.   (travel, traveled)

5. Circle the nouns in the sentence.

Our class cannot wait to wear our costumes for the play.

6. Write another word that has the spelling pattern -*ow* as in *pillow*.

_____

1. Ⓨ Ⓝ

2. Ⓨ Ⓝ

3. Ⓨ Ⓝ

4. Ⓨ Ⓝ

5. Ⓨ Ⓝ

6. Ⓨ Ⓝ

___ / 6
Total

NAME: _____ DATE: _____

DIRECTIONS Read and answer each question.

1. Ⓨ Ⓝ

1. Add quotation marks to the sentence.
....

Dad asked, Are we going to have time to go to the track meet?

2. Ⓨ Ⓝ

2. Write *the scarf that Fiona is wearing* in another way.

_____

3. Ⓨ Ⓝ

3. Write a sentence to describe a classmate. Circle the adjectives.

_____

4. Ⓨ Ⓝ

_____

5. Ⓨ Ⓝ

4. Write two adjectives about winter weather where you live.

_____   _____

6. Ⓨ Ⓝ

___ / 6
Total

5. Write the correct verb to complete the sentence.
....

Alex is not _____ a good day, and he wants to go home.   (have, had, having)
....

6. Circle the word that is spelled correctly.
....

roial

royal

royel

NAME: _____ **DATE:** _____

DIRECTIONS Read and answer each question.

1. Circle the words that need capital letters.

I would like to publish my poem titled "rainy days" in our class poetry book.

1. Ⓨ Ⓝ

2. Ⓨ Ⓝ

2. Add apostrophes to the sentence.

The neighbors house is very scary, so Tanners mom helped us get our ball back.

3. Ⓨ Ⓝ

4. Ⓨ Ⓝ

3. Write the correct pronoun to complete the sentence.

Maya and Anna wanted to put on _____ bathing suits and run in the sprinklers. (their, his, her)

5. Ⓨ Ⓝ

6. Ⓨ Ⓝ

4. Write two adjectives about your favorite book.

_____   _____

___ / 6
Total

5. Write an adjective to complete the sentence.

I do not like to see snakes because they are _____ to me.

6. Write another word that has the spelling pattern -oy as in *joy*.

_____

NAME: _____ **DATE:** _____

SCORE

DIRECTIONS Read and answer each question.

1. (Y)(N)

1. Write a sentence about a special place you enjoy going to. Be sure to include a comma.

_____

2. (Y)(N)

_____

3. (Y)(N)

2. Write *the bottle belonging to the baby* in another way.

_____

4. (Y)(N)

3. Which part of speech describes a noun?

5. (Y)(N)

verb   adjective   adverb

6. (Y)(N)

4. Write a noun to complete the sentence.

___ / 6
Total

The _____ hiked quickly up the mountain to make it to the top.

5. Circle the past tense form of the word *find*.

finded   finding   found

6. Circle the word that is spelled correctly.

mowth   mouth   mowthe

NAME: _____ **DATE:** _____

| DIRECTIONS | Read and answer each question. |

1. Circle the words that need capital letters.

Wade announced, "The theater is finally showing the movie *truck race*!"

1. Ⓨ Ⓝ

2. Ⓨ Ⓝ

2. Use an apostrophe to write *the new jeans that belong to Christina* in another way.

_____

3. Ⓨ Ⓝ

3. Write a verb to complete the sentence.

Parker _____ he heard something outside the tent.

4. Ⓨ Ⓝ

5. Ⓨ Ⓝ

4. Write an adverb to complete the sentence.

Jacob skated _____ at the park until his mother told him to come home.

6. Ⓨ Ⓝ

___/ 6
Total

5. Circle the adjectives in the sentence.

The bright light kept us up at night.

6. Add the *pre-* prefix to the base word *school*. Write the word on the line.

_____

NAME: _____ DATE: _____

SCORE

DIRECTIONS Read and answer each question.

1. Ⓨ Ⓝ

1. Write a make-believe address for a book character. Be sure to include correct punctuation.

_____

2. Ⓨ Ⓝ

_____

3. Ⓨ Ⓝ

2. Add quotation marks and a comma to the sentence.

Ava asked Can I have a little more time to work on
my assignment?

4. Ⓨ Ⓝ

5. Ⓨ Ⓝ

3. Write the correct pronoun that makes sense in the sentence.

6. Ⓨ Ⓝ

The dog enjoys _____ meal when no one is near the food.
(their, its, our)

___ / 6
Total

4. Write two adjectives about summer vacation.

_____   _____

5. Write the correct verb to complete the sentence.

My baby sister _____ still learning how to walk.
(is, am, are)

6. Add the *un-* prefix to the base word *cover*. Write the word on the line.

_____

NAME: _____ **DATE:** _____

DIRECTIONS Read and answer each question.

1. Write a sentence of dialogue that a coach would say to his or her team before a big game. Be sure to include a comma and quotation marks.

_____

_____

2. Use an apostrophe to write *the spark from the fire* in another way.

_____

3. Write a sentence using the word *dedication.*

_____

_____

4. Write two adverbs to complete the sentence.

The spaceship departed _____ and _____ from the landing strip.

5. Circle the past tense form of the word *get*.

getted   got   getting

6. Write a word that includes the *-ness* spelling pattern as in *darkness*.

_____

1. Ⓨ Ⓝ
2. Ⓨ Ⓝ
3. Ⓨ Ⓝ
4. Ⓨ Ⓝ
5. Ⓨ Ⓝ
6. Ⓨ Ⓝ

___ / 6
Total

NAME: _____ **DATE:** _____

1. Ⓨ Ⓝ

2. Ⓨ Ⓝ

3. Ⓨ Ⓝ

4. Ⓨ Ⓝ

5. Ⓨ Ⓝ

6. Ⓨ Ⓝ

___ / 6
Total

DIRECTIONS Read and answer each question.

1. Add a city and state to the following address. Be sure to include correct punctuation.

1299 Adams Street

_____ _____ 49033

2. Add quotation marks to the sentence.

Mom commented, I thought your friends
were all polite at your party.

3. Write the correct verb to complete the sentence.

The children _____ playing a game of tag together.
          (is, was, were)

4. Circle the adverb in the sentence.

The clock ticked continually throughout the day.

5. Write the past tense form of the word *hear* on the line.

I _____ that the rules on the playground
have changed.

6. Write a word that includes the *-tion* spelling pattern as in *creation*.

_____

NAME: _____ **DATE:** _____

DIRECTIONS Read and answer each question.

1. Circle the words in the sentence that need capital letters.

Carla remembers her dad singing a song titled "school days" to her.

1. Ⓨ Ⓝ

2. Add quotation marks to the sentence.

Do you think I should go to the party? Marty wondered.

2. Ⓨ Ⓝ

3. Ⓨ Ⓝ

3. Write the correct pronoun to complete the sentence.

4. Ⓨ Ⓝ

Cindy loved _____ sister a lot, but they still fought.
(their, his, her)

5. Ⓨ Ⓝ

6. Ⓨ Ⓝ

4. Write two adjectives about your home.

_____   _____

___ / 6
Total

5. Write the correct verb to complete the sentence.

I may _____ friends out on the playground, but I
(seeing, saw, see)

still want to be alone.

6. Write a word that includes the *-sion* spelling pattern as in *decision*.

_____

NAME: _____ DATE: _____

SCORE

DIRECTIONS Read and answer each question.

1. Ⓨ Ⓝ

1. Add a city and state to the following address. Be sure to include correct punctuation.

1834 Grant Court

2. Ⓨ Ⓝ

_____ _____ 98774

3. Ⓨ Ⓝ

2. Write *the toothbrush belonging to Lucas* in another way.

_____

4. Ⓨ Ⓝ

3. Write a sentence using the word *luxury*.

_____

5. Ⓨ Ⓝ

_____

6. Ⓨ Ⓝ

4. Write two adjectives about your best friend.

_____ _____

___ / 6
Total

5. Write the correct verb to complete the sentence.

Principal Anderson _____ in our classroom to observe.   (stay, staying, stayed)

6. Write a word that includes the *-ful* spelling pattern as in *careful*.

_____

NAME: _____ DATE: _____

DIRECTIONS Read and answer each question.

1. Write the name of a place you would like to visit using correct capitalization.

_____

1. Ⓨ Ⓝ

2. Ⓨ Ⓝ

2. Add quotation marks to the sentence.

What is on the menu for school lunch today? Nick wondered.

3. Ⓨ Ⓝ

3. Write a sentence to compare two pets. Use adjectives that end in *-er*.

_____

_____

4. Ⓨ Ⓝ

5. Ⓨ Ⓝ

4. Circle the past tense verb in the sentence.

The athlete wanted to win the trophy.

6. Ⓨ Ⓝ

___ / 6
Total

5. Circle the pronouns in the sentence.

We must protect ourselves by always wearing bike helmets.

6. Circle the word that is spelled correctly.

aisland

eyeland

island

NAME: _____ **DATE:** _____

DIRECTIONS Read and answer each question.

1. Write a sentence of dialogue that a teacher might say to his or her class. Be sure to include correct punctuation.

_____

_____

_____

2. Use an apostrophe to write *the wing of the airplane* in another way.

_____

3. Circle the nouns in the sentence.

The lion is stalking and looking for its next meal.

4. Write two adjectives about football.

_____   _____

5. Write the correct verb to complete the sentence.

I may _____ a bald eagle on our hike today.
          (saw, seeing, see)

6. Write a word that includes the *-le* spelling pattern as in *single*.

_____

NAME: _____ **DATE:** _____

DIRECTIONS Read and answer each question.

1. Circle the words in the sentence that need capital letters.

I used to love the song "this old man" when I was little.

2. Add apostrophes to the sentence.

Jimmys pet snake and Kens pet hamster should never be left in the same cage!

3. Circle the past tense verb in the sentence.

Brad left his water bottle on the playground.

4. Write an adverb to complete the sentence.

The baseball team worked _____ all year long.

5. Write a sentence using the word *calm*.

_____

_____

6. Circle the word that is spelled correctly.

settel   settle   settul

1. Ⓨ Ⓝ

2. Ⓨ Ⓝ

3. Ⓨ Ⓝ

4. Ⓨ Ⓝ

5. Ⓨ Ⓝ

6. Ⓨ Ⓝ

___ / 6
Total

NAME: _____ DATE: _____

DIRECTIONS Read and answer each question.

1. Write a sentence about a place you visit frequently. Be sure to include a comma.

_____

_____

2. Add quotation marks and a comma to the sentence.

Mr. Scott, I really wish you would be my teacher again next year   Ezra said.

3. Write a sentence to compare two family members. Use adjectives that end in -er.

_____

_____

4. Write an adjective to complete the sentence.

The man's _____ eyes were the color of the sky.

5. Circle the past tense form of the word *lose*.

losing   lost   loose

6. Write a word that includes the -er spelling pattern as in *camper*.

_____

NAME: _____ DATE: _____

DIRECTIONS Read and answer each question.

1. Circle the words in the sentence that need capital letters.

Ben likes to talk to other kids online about the video game *power works*.

2. Use an apostrophe to write *the car belonging to my dad* in another way.

_____

3. Write the correct pronoun to complete the sentence.

Marcus does not want _____ swimsuit to be too tight.
(he, his, you)

4. Circle the verbs in sentence A below.

5. Underline the adverb in sentence A below.

A The tall skyscraper looked as if it gently touched the clouds.

6. Circle the word that is spelled correctly.

leeder

leader

leider

1. Ⓨ Ⓝ

2. Ⓨ Ⓝ

3. Ⓨ Ⓝ

4. Ⓨ Ⓝ

5. Ⓨ Ⓝ

6. Ⓨ Ⓝ

___ / 6
Total

NAME: _____ **DATE:** _____

DIRECTIONS Read and answer each question.

1. Write the name of a poem you like. Be sure to include capital letters.

_____

2. Write the correct verb to complete the sentence.

Our family always struggles to _____ on a restaurant for dinner.   (deciding, decided, decide)

3. Circle the adjectives in the sentence.

The sun is bright today.

4. Circle the past tense verb in the sentence.

The librarian helped me to find the perfect book.

5. Write the correct verb to complete the sentence.

Annemarie _____ with her friends in the audience to watch the play.   (sitting, sat, sitted)

6. Circle the word that is spelled correctly.

babys   babees   babies

NAME: _____ DATE: _____

DIRECTIONS Read and answer each question.

1. Write a sentence of dialogue that a mother might say to a child at bedtime. Be sure to include correct punctuation.

_____

_____

_____

2. Write a sentence about an object your friend owns using an apostrophe.

_____

_____

3. Circle the past tense verbs in the sentence.

I sat when I worked at the computer so that I felt comfortable.

4. Write an adverb to complete the sentence.

Megan worked _____ to finish her homework on time.

5. Circle the past tense form of the word *begin*.

begins   beginning   began

6. Circle the word that is spelled correctly.

lim   limm   limb

1. Ⓨ Ⓝ

2. Ⓨ Ⓝ

3. Ⓨ Ⓝ

4. Ⓨ Ⓝ

5. Ⓨ Ⓝ

6. Ⓨ Ⓝ

___ / 6
Total

NAME: _____ **DATE:** _____

DIRECTIONS Read and answer each question.

1. (Y)(N)

1. Add a city and state to the following address. Be sure to include correct punctuation.

....

99 Thornwood Drive

2. (Y)(N)

_____ _____ 94563

....

3. (Y)(N)

2. Use apostrophes to compare two characteristics of your classmates. (Ex: Sophia's hair is brown, and Nora's hair is black.)

4. (Y)(N)

_____

_____

5. (Y)(N)

3. Circle the past tense verb in the sentence.

....

6. (Y)(N)

The prize for the contest was a ticket to Adventure Time Park.

....

___ / 6
Total

4. Write the correct adverb to complete the sentence.

....

Anita learned how to _____ measure objects with
a ruler.   (precisely, fairly, fast)

....

5. Write the past tense form of the word *drive* to complete the sentence.

....

Who _____ us home from tennis practice last week?

....

6. Write a word that includes the *-less* spelling pattern as in *careless*.

_____

NAME: _____ **DATE:** _____

DIRECTIONS Read and answer each question.

1. Write the name of a nearby town using correct capitalization.

_____

1. Ⓨ Ⓝ

2. Write *the house belonging to my neighbor* in another way.

_____

2. Ⓨ Ⓝ

3. Ⓨ Ⓝ

3. Rewrite the sentence in past tense.

Martin and Will will hike up to the waterfall, and they will see a lot of wildlife.

_____

_____

4. Ⓨ Ⓝ

5. Ⓨ Ⓝ

6. Ⓨ Ⓝ

4. Circle the adjectives in sentence A below.

5. Underline the adverb in sentence A below.

A I generously used red and blue paint on the canvas.

___ / 6
Total

6. Write a word that includes the *pre-*spelling pattern as in *prepare*.

_____

NAME: _____ **DATE:** _____

Read and answer each question.

SCORE

1. (Y)(N)

2. (Y)(N)

3. (Y)(N)

4. (Y)(N)

5. (Y)(N)

6. (Y)(N)

___ / 6
Total

1. Add a comma to the following address.

49300 West Kingston Road

Newport Beach CA 98800

2. Use apostrophes to compare two objects that belong to your classmates. (Ex: Hector's coat looks much warmer than Rodrigo's coat.)

_____

_____

3. Circle the adjectives in the sentence.

Adventurous Anna likes to observe the slimy worms that live in wet soil.

4. Many plural nouns end in *-s* or *-es*. Circle the noun that does **not** follow this rule.

man   worm   plant

5. Circle the adverb in the sentence.

Ruby endlessly worked on her art project until it was complete.

6. Write a word that includes the *un-* spelling pattern as in *unknown*.

_____

NAME: _____ **DATE:** _____

DIRECTIONS Read and answer each question.

1. Write a sentence of dialogue that a principal might say at an assembly. Be sure to include a comma and quotation marks.

_____

_____

_____

2. Write *the body part of an animal* in another way.

_____

3. Circle the pronoun in the sentence.

Chloe loves to play with her dog at the park.

4. Circle the nouns in the sentence.

The third graders were not allowed to leave the cafeteria because they were so noisy.

5. Write the correct verb to complete the sentence.

We were so _____ of ourselves for reaching our goal.
(pride, proud, proudly)

6. Write a word that includes the *re-* spelling pattern as in *redo*.

_____

1. Ⓨ Ⓝ

2. Ⓨ Ⓝ

3. Ⓨ Ⓝ

4. Ⓨ Ⓝ

5. Ⓨ Ⓝ

6. Ⓨ Ⓝ

___ / 6
Total

NAME: _____ **DATE:** _____

DIRECTIONS Read and answer each question.

1. Circle the item that will always be capitalized.

movie titles   adjectives   words with
                                           apostrophes

2. Write *the baseball that belongs to Michael* in another way.

_____

3. Circle the adjectives in the sentence.

Justin likes to wear a comfortable, green coat.

4. Write two adjectives about your favorite dessert.

_____   _____

5. Write the correct verb to complete the sentence.

I can _____ a flock of seagulls at the beach.
        (see, saw, seen)

6. Write a word that includes the *-er* spelling pattern as in *faster*.

_____

NAME: _____ DATE: _____

DIRECTIONS Read and answer each question.

1. Circle the words that need capital letters.

"I hope our choir does not have to learn 'this train's a-coming' because it's a silly song," Greta complained.

2. Add apostrophes to the sentence.

Lances handbook tells the scouts that their troops destination is miles away.

3. Write a sentence using the word *failure.*

_____

_____

4. Write the correct adverb that makes sense in the sentence.

The ballet dancers moved _____ during the recital.
(gracefully, angrily)

5. Write the correct verb to complete the sentence.

The litter of kittens _____ so cute to look at yesterday.
(are, was, were)

6. Write a word that includes the *-est* spelling pattern as in *biggest.*

_____

1. Ⓨ Ⓝ

2. Ⓨ Ⓝ

3. Ⓨ Ⓝ

4. Ⓨ Ⓝ

5. Ⓨ Ⓝ

6. Ⓨ Ⓝ

___ / 6
Total

ANSWER KEY

Day 1
1. "The dog has not been fed yet," my mother told us.
2. Frank yelled, "We are the state champions!"
3. walked, make
4. quickly
5. The, the, beautiful
6. cries

Day 2
1. 1700 Lakeview Place
   Springfield, OR 99810
2. The Zookeeper's Job
3. Answers will vary.
4. felt
5. his
6. tapped

Day 3
1. Answers will vary.
2. "**Bicycle Built** for **Two**"
3. I walked to school every day.
4. I will walk to school every day.
5. fall
6. writing

Day 4
1. "I don't want to have salad for dinner," moaned Jeremy.
2. "I want to go see the parade downtown," said Gus.
3. Our, big, brown, furry
4. knowledge
5. men
6. happiness

Day 5
1. "Please don't take anything out of my desk," Paul said.
2. "Where should we go for dinner tonight?" wondered Alice.
3. nicest
4. more often
5. sheep
6. motion

Day 6
1. Henry's dog likes to run.
2. 12 Hancock Avenue
   Princeville, FL 65291
3. Doreen wants to go to the baseball game, **but** she also wants to go swimming.
4. Answers will vary.
5. her
6. dropped

Day 7
1. Frances's book was due today at the library.
2. "Here is the book I was telling you about," said Heather.
3. or
4. sweeter
5. Answers will vary.
6. spotting

Day 8
1. José's friend
2. 723 Pine Road
   Grant Falls, GA 09221
3. yet
4. more quietly
5. Answers will vary.
6. needed

Day 9
1. Lily's mother wanted to drive on the field trip.
2. my teacher's chair
3. so
4. often
5. dressed
6. lately

Day 10
1. Evan's bike
2. 11 Veneto Road
   Virginia City, VA 75400
3. blue, cotton, red
4. began
5. I **moved** to a new home and **started** a new school.
6. really

Day 11
1. I wanted to read **A Princess Tale**, which is the sequel book to **The Castle** in the **Sky**.
2. 4439 Parkson Road
   Bridgetown, NH 45200
3. Answers will vary.
4. The, loud, the, busy
5. had
6. brightness

Day 12
1. Answers will vary.
2. "I cannot wait for the school play tomorrow," said Ava.
3. I **wrote** in my journal every day.
4. I **will write** in my journal every day.
5. Mona said that **her** dinner portion was too big to eat.
6. finding

ANSWER KEY *(cont.)*

Day 13
1. Answers will vary.
2. "The birthday party is going to start on time," said Paulina.
3. her
4. smarter
5. water
6. bushes

Day 14
1. Stephanie's brother was not behaving at dinner.
2. "That music is making my head hurt," Francisco complained.
3. is
4. burned
5. My sister never wants to share **her** toys with me.
6. benches

Day 15
1. I don't know where Lucy's library book might be.
2. Lucas shouted, "Let's run out to the playground before anyone else!"
3. Answers will vary.
4. has
5. The, brown, the, sandy
6. tracks

Day 16
1. Jason's friend was trying to organize a kickball game.
2. "My mom will buy us pizza at the party," Charlie explained.
3. are
4. The, large, smaller
5. People
6. berry

Day 17
1. Ted's lunch box was in the lost and found.
2. Gus explained, "I was late for school because the alarm did not go off."
3. Answers will vary.
4. foot
5. Mary
6. muddy

Day 18
1. Rita's dog
2. 1650 Warner Road New York**,** NY 12112
3. unruly, her
4. played
5. angrier
6. smiled

Day 19
1. Hector's baby brother
2. Answers will vary.
3. has, find
4. Mom watched Henry to make sure **he** was playing nicely with **his** friend.
5. did, was, scared
6. matches

Day 20
1. Desi's birthday party
2. Jacob's aunt was not able to bring Jacob's cousin to the party.
3. The lake **dried** up because there **was** not enough rain this season.
4. quickly
5. his
6. riches

Day 21
1. Roman's tooth
2. 544 Hancock Lane West Franklin**,** IL 68221
3. are, eat
4. Answers will vary.
5. bought
6. happen

Day 22
1. 1812 Harding Court Clayton**,** PA 98850
2. Hank commented, "I wish that I could have a cupcake."
3. Answers will vary.
4. slowly
5. My, excited, the
6. swimming

Day 23
1. the car's tire
2. "I like to drink my tea while it is hot," Grandma explained.
3. have
4. tomorrow, homework, school
5. I can order cheese pizza**, or** I can order pepperoni pizza.
6. unclear

Day 24
1. the map's picture
2. The librarian found me the book that I wanted, titled **Abe Lincoln's Boyhood**.
3. often
4. so
5. shook
6. against

ANSWER KEY (cont.)

Day 25

1. 12 Brookhurst
   West Covington**,** KY 29930
2. Jack's mom was not able to help us with our homework, so we worked together.
3. her
4. angrily
5. got
6. erupt

Day 26

1. My friend recommends reading **The Mystery Solver** by Hank Williams.
2. "All of our animals have been rescued by our staff**,**" explained the zookeeper.
3. is
4. The school day was over**,** **but** the bus was still not there.
5. teeth, cavities
6. stitch

Day 27

1. Michael's barbecue
2. Mr. Franklin's work
3. Answers will vary.
4. sheep
5. playfully
6. crawl

Day 28

1. The radio just played my favorite song, "**Missing You**."
2. 701 Kenton Road
   Berkeley**,** CA 88720
3. quickly
4. Adverbs are words that describe verbs and nouns.
5. fanciest
6. hotter

Day 29

1. Roberto's video game
2. "Our family gathering was a lot of fun**!**" Anna exclaimed.
3. The mother bear was trying to take care of **her** cubs.
4. Answers will vary.
5. The snow was falling all day**,** **and** the neighborhood was quiet.
6. saddest

Day 30

1. I read the poem "**Gray Day at the Beach**," aloud to the class.
2. 229 Adams Road
   West Palm Beach**,** FL 88720
3. Answers will vary.
4. I, our
5. Mom wanted to take all of the kids to the beach**,** **but** it was raining.
6. knight

Day 31

1. Answers will vary.
2. Oscar's lunch
3. Answers will vary.
4. The, green, the, warm
5. The **sharks** swim through the water for food.
6. shortly

Day 32

1. My favorite movie is titled, *Beauty and the Beast*.
2. "The video was a lot of fun to make**!**" Kevin exclaimed.
3. **Before** I go to school, I eat my breakfast.
4. hotter
5. happily
6. changing

Day 33

1. I have been wondering if the title **A Doomsday Mystery** means the book will be scary.
2. Heather's homework was not inside her backpack.
3. Leslie played on the playground**,** **and** her mom came to get her.
4. Answers will vary.
5. Answers will vary.
6. leaves

Day 34

1. Lin wondered**,** "Why has our teacher been absent all week?"
2. the flower's petal
3. eats
4. Answers will vary.
5. Answers will vary.
6. mainly

Day 35

1. "Please do not eat food in the museum**,**" the employee warned the students.
2. Jackson's sister was always following us around.
3. her, her
4. safely
5. Mean kids at the playground **act** like bullies and **tease** us.
6. halves

Day 36

1. I think I may sing the song titled "**A Starry Night**" for the talent show.
2. the coat's pockets
3. strolled, looked
4. the, speeding, our, quiet
5. **Since** the weather is nice, I can go swimming outside.
6. placement

ANSWER KEY (cont.)

Day 37

1. The radio station always plays the song titled "**Feeling Silly** and **Funky**."
2. My neighbor's swimming pool felt very refreshing on a hot day.
3. My uncle flew into town and brought two suitcases with **him**.
4. man
5. Answers will vary.
6. aging

Day 38

1. 80 Broadway Avenue Parklane, MT 68868
2. the planet's ring
3. The driver got in his car and drove to **his** mom's house.
4. although
5. moves
6. larger

Day 39

1. 1220 Irving Lane Santa Maria, CA 99093
2. the black bear's cub
3. helps
4. Answers will vary.
5. Answers will vary.
6. worry

Day 40

1. 14 Grant Court Highland, CO 75900
2. Joshua's story was written in a week during writing time.
3. He likes to ride **his** skateboard to school.
4. cheerfully
5. smallest
6. hurry

Day 41

1. Should we dance to the song "**Party People**" or the song "**From My Heart**"?
2. I am looking for the hotel in Paris, France.
3. The students from Parker School **will be** picking up litter.
4. A, healthy, sunflower, green
5. books
6. planned

Day 42

1. The books **Over the Deep End** and **Under the Bridge** are both written by the same author.
2. Santiago is trying to save money to visit his family in Albuquerque, New Mexico.
3. The fly **buzzed** around the kitchen.
4. child
5. excitedly
6. happiness

Day 43

1. I heard the song "**Friends Forever**" in the movie *Girls' Day Out.*
2. Chloe's backyard has the best tree house I have ever seen!
3. Sasha's mother was not happy about the squirrels in **her** garden.
4. The astronomer **watched** the meteor shower in the sky.
5. hopes, make
6. city

Day 44

1. The title of the video game is *Speed Demon*.
2. Sofia's pet
3. I **go** to the library every day during summer vacation.
4. Answers will vary.
5. held, got dressed
6. sigh

Day 45

1. "That is the new student in our class," remarked Cara.
2. Maria's ears felt funny on the airplane, and Mother's ears also did not feel normal.
3. The, pretty, the
4. evenly
5. fly
6. swimming

Day 46

1. The book I wish I could read next is **The Baseball Hero**.
2. The babysitter's mistake was saying yes to a snowball fight.
3. her
4. The, warm, the, our, special
5. Answers will vary.
6. almost

Day 47

1. Rosie's soccer uniform was mixed up with her sister's uniform.
2. Hank's food
3. new
4. mouse
5. lovingly, quickly
6. dragged

ANSWER KEY *(cont.)*

Day 48

1. I hope that we can go on vacation to New Orleans**,** Louisiana.
2. 90 Torrey Road Vancouver**,** WA 98330
3. ring
4. Answers will vary.
5. jumped
6. celebration

Day 49

1. 778 Hanover Street Honolulu**,** HI 78944
2. Pablo's computer
3. walking
4. Answers will vary.
5. her
6. spotting

Day 50

1. Who knows the words to the song "**Summertime Blues**"?
2. The teacher's students were quiet while they listened to Mrs. Walter's directions.
3. means
4. happily
5. his
6. soap

Day 51

1. Mason and I watched the movie *Family Time* together.
2. Maria's sister wanted to go to school with her.
3. Answers will vary.
4. The, curious, the, loud, blinking
5. he
6. rotting

Day 52

1. The video game I want for my birthday is called *Digging up the Ruins*.
2. Samantha's leg
3. tallest
4. I **saw** the customer pay for the groceries at the store.
5. quietly, peacefully
6. plainly

Day 53

1. Fernando's computer
2. 11 Jackson Blvd. Oakland**,** UT 65710
3. My backpack was in my locker**, but** my homework was still missing.
4. her
5. will
6. hoping

Day 54

1. Sunit had to move with her family to Orlando**,** Florida.
2. the hero's cape
3. loudest
4. Answers will vary.
5. Answers will vary.
6. mainly

Day 55

1. My grandparents traveled to our home from **Phoenix, Arizona**.
2. 88 Easter Street Xenia**,** IL 88900
3. though
4. Answers will vary.
5. The **children** were not able to hear the teacher's directions.
6. couple

Day 56

1. My family loves to go on vacation to **San Francisco, California**.
2. 54 Hawthorne Street Carson**,** NV 88900
3. The school bus was late to pick us up**, so** we were late to class.
4. her, fluffy, a, stormy
5. ate, had
6. napping

Day 57

1. The post office delivers to **Newberg, Washington**, and across the border at **Hillsborough, Oregon**.
2. Lily's coat
3. Answers will vary.
4. luckier
5. quickly
6. scent

Day 58

1. "I know all of the words to the song, '**That Pretty Little Rainbow**,'" bragged Julie.
2. Jack's baseball team won the championship, and they all received trophies!
3. read
4. Lucy
5. you, our, we
6. creation

Day 59

1. "Who is going to help me collect homework?" the teacher asked.
2. the scientist's tools
3. although
4. Answers will vary.
5. Answers will vary.
6. weigh

ANSWER KEY (cont.)

Day 60

1. "Why am I always the last one to get picked for the team?" Liam complained.
2. Alex's birthday invitation list includes Oscar's sister.
3. Answers will vary.
4. Answers will vary.
5. men
6. immigration

Day 61

1. Answers will vary.
2. a friend's pet
3. The baby will go to bed **as long as** she has her bottle first.
4. Answers will vary.
5. museums
6. chair

Day 62

1. Destiny and Brittany wanted to visit Rome**,** Italy**,** together.
2. Mom's hair
3. girl, house, day
4. Answers will vary.
5. loudly
6. where

Day 63

1. At the roller rink, they played the song "**Stop Causing Trouble**."
2. Tracy's ice cream
3. women
4. spend
5. We should see the orca whales in the ocean**, but** we may have an unlucky day.
6. tapping

Day 64

1. 46577 Parkview Place Seattle**,** WA 59004
2. Oliver's toy car
3. find
4. desk
5. secretly
6. corner

Day 65

1. 490 Whitehaven Road Dallas**,** TX 40399
2. Sarah's game was rained out and rescheduled for tomorrow.
3. and
4. hid
5. The **children** love going to summer camp each year.
6. before

Day 66

1. I think that the poem titled "**The Wind Calls My Name**" is very beautiful.
2. Martin's favorite hobby is collecting stamps and coins.
3. play
4. The, yellow, the, damp
5. The **women** read books to relax on their vacation.
6. baking

Day 67

1. Kassie is trying to learn how to play "**When** the **Sun Comes Up**" on the piano.
2. Ted's candy
3. Answers will vary.
4. call
5. soon
6. worthiness

Day 68

1. There are many desert wildflowers near Phoenix**,** Arizona.
2. Jackson's skateboard was brand new and a lot of fun to ride.
3. Answers will vary.
4. children, men, women, teeth
5. woke
6. competition

Day 69

1. 5550 Arrowhead Way Lake Tahoe**,** CA 89772
2. Ava's water
3. lose
4. Answers will vary.
5. Answers will vary.
6. lately

Day 70

1. Answers will vary.
2. Harper's dog was not getting along with Maya's dog.
3. Answers will vary.
4. she, her
5. The **men** played football at the park all morning.
6. suddenly

Day 71

1. It is difficult to play the song "**Stomping Along**" on the piano.
2. the store's owner
3. The hummingbird **flapped** its wings very quickly.
4. The, blue, a, thick, the, hot
5. teeth
6. sadness

ANSWER KEY *(cont.)*

Day 72

1. How many syllables are in the haiku poem titled "**The Beautiful Forest**"?
2. "I prefer pepperoni pizza over cheese pizza**,**" replied Claire.
3. old
4. stay
5. shyly
6. thinner

Day 73

1. "Hey Mom, I just noticed that the video game titled ***Baseball Championship*** is on sale," said Rodrigo.
2. The moving van was traveling from Houston**,** Texas**,** to Miami**,** Florida.
3. **Jacob's** football was missing, so **Walter's** mom looked for it in the garage.
4. was, hurt, fell
5. Our class picnic **will take** place on Friday afternoon.
6. kinder

Day 74

1. 6855 Hawthorne Road Portland**,** OR 90222
2. Jayden's report card
3. and
4. Answers will vary.
5. told
6. safest

Day 75

1. "This homework is taking too long**,**" complained Nate.
2. Don't you want to go to Milo's party to celebrate Milo's birthday?
3. harder
4. slowly
5. Jack and Carol **walked** to the swimming pool together.
6. shipment

Day 76

1. the classroom's door
2. "That construction work woke me up too early**,**" complained Dad.
3. Answers will vary.
4. The, happy, his, young, the, amusement
5. Liam's **feet** were hurting after stepping on glass.
6. nearer

Day 77

1. 650 Jackson Street Templeton**,** NC 69440
2. "I think that Grandpa laughs the most at his own jokes," Chris said.
3. The leash on the dog **will be** too tight, so June **will loosen** it.
4. tooth
5. calmly, repeatedly
6. funnier

Day 78

1. There are many old buildings in Rome**,** Italy**,** and Berlin**,** Germany.
2. The dog's fleas made him scratch.
3. The whale **came** up from the water and **poked** its nose in the air.
4. Answers will vary.
5. our, family, the, closest, the
6. preheat

Day 79

1. "I am not sure if I want to go to the slumber party**,**" Ellen said.
2. the table's edge
3. quietly
4. He
5. The, lifelong, the, soccer
6. easiest

Day 80

1. Answers will vary.
2. Harry isn't afraid of Peter's dog, but he is afraid of Peter's brother.
3. the, the, fast
4. tightly
5. No one **will come** to the soccer practice because of the rain.
6. unlucky

Day 81

1. 4430 Northwest 50th Street New York**,** NY 89220
2. the phone's buttons
3. Answers will vary.
4. The, shiny, the, sandy
5. The **men** boarded the bus after the women got on.
6. smallest

Day 82

1. Mrs. Sanchez remarked**,** "I am proud of how hard you all worked today."
2. Dana's dance recital
3. ran, played
4. tooth
5. quietly, deeply
6. untie

Day 83

1. Gus's backpack
2. My dad yelled**,** "Be careful riding your bike on the street!"
3. The, small, white, our, favorite, the
4. our
5. reddest
6. sillier

#51168—*180 Days of Language* © Shell Education

ANSWER KEY *(cont.)*

Day 84
1. Answers will vary.
2. Wade's apple
3. Answers will vary.
4. Answers will vary.
5. wonderful
6. quietness

Day 85
1. The lifeguard shouted, "It's break time, so you need to get out of the pool!"
2. A giraffe's neck helps it to reach food in tall trees.
3. extremely
4. sat
5. The **women** ate lunch in the lunchroom and then returned to their desks.
6. tough

Day 86
1. Is that a piano that plays in the background of the song "**Move Your Body**"?
2. Jack's bike
3. tallest
4. Diego, soup, dinner
5. The loose tooth **fell** out.
6. Answers will vary.

Day 87
1. I loved listening to my teacher read poetry aloud, especially the poem titled "**Waves Crashing Silently**."
2. The hot water burned Kerry's hand.
3. Rita's toy **was** so real looking that people **were** surprised it **was** a doll.
4. children, mice
5. anxiously
6. Answers will vary.

Day 88
1. 440 Hancock Way
   Oklahoma City, OK 60550
2. "We can help endangered species in many ways," the scientist explained.
3. a, big, trading
4. he
5. Answers will vary.
6. fitness

Day 89
1. "Look who came to school wearing a new skirt," remarked Candace.
2. the hippopotamus's wrinkles
3. often
4. Answers will vary.
5. took
6. payment

Day 90
1. Where is Milwaukee, Wisconsin, on the map?
2. She's always safe on her sister's bike, but she is not used to riding her brother's scooter.
3. shiniest
4. happily
5. children
6. valuable

Day 91
1. Should we sing "**Love You Forever**" as a trio or as a duet?
2. Olivia's dress
3. Answers will vary.
4. Yummy, delicious
5. The big white **geese** lived on the farm.
6. Answers will vary.

Day 92
1. 3009 Hartford Road
   Chicago, IL 75884
2. Sophia's bike
3. Answers will vary.
4. deer
5. daily
6. reread

Day 93
1. Answers will vary.
2. "Who should be the line leader today?" Paul asked his teacher.
3. black
4. The, young, the, rock
5. excitedly, loudly
6. tight

Day 94
1. Answers will vary.
2. "How much longer until lunch?" Sam complained.
3. colder
4. Answers will vary.
5. wrote
6. Answers will vary.

Day 95
1. song titles
2. The ship's captain can't stop working while sailing because it is the captain's job.
3. Answers will vary.
4. The, long, the, wet
5. slowly
6. Answers will vary.

Day 96
1. I think I know all of the words to the song "**Uncle John's Farm**."
2. Erik's drum set
3. fastest
4. muffin, pancakes
5. quickly, sneakily
6. Answers will vary.

ANSWER KEY *(cont.)*

Day 97
1. "I am very excited for the holiday parade today!" exclaimed Rosa.
2. José's water bottle
3. needed
4. goose
5. quietly, quickly
6. Answers will vary.

Day 98
1. Answers will vary.
2. Would you like to go to Hank's house or Jesse's house after school?
3. Answers will vary.
4. The, grocery, closer, my, the, basketball
5. feel
6. funnier

Day 99
1. 4009 Tellium Lane Jacksonville, FL 89403
2. the book's last chapter
3. wrap
4. Answers will vary.
5. the, loudest, the, entire
6. cuter

Day 100
1. titles of poems
2. The bear's cub wandered off from the pack, but the cub's mother kept a close eye on him.
3. him
4. quietly
5. Answers will vary.
6. Answers will vary.

Day 101
1. The movie *Norm's Day Out* made me laugh very hard!
2. the backpack's pocket
3. funnier
4. The, small, blue, the, low
5. Lily's **teeth** were wiggly and about to fall out.
6. Answers will vary.

Day 102
1. The movie *Earthquake Time* is supposed to be very scary.
2. Seth's pencil
3. Kai's notebook **was** missing from his backpack.
4. child
5. usually, happily
6. burst

Day 103
1. My mom bought me the video game *Race Day*, and it is a fun game.
2. "Let's take Buster to the dog park," Brady said.
3. or
4. packed
5. quickly
6. certain

Day 104
1. holidays
2. the bike's basket
3. Evan had to go to soccer practice, **but** he didn't want to go.
4. Answers will vary.
5. Eric, Sam, sandwiches, lunch
6. replace

Day 105
1. I love the dog character in the movie *The Cat's Meow*.
2. Carter's coach thought that Carter's performance could have been better.
3. happy
4. quickly
5. is
6. Answers will vary.

Day 106
1. Buffalo, New York, is where my grandparents live.
2. the city's high school
3. kind
4. The, yellow, school, the
5. safely
6. quietest

Day 107
1. Our music teacher helped us write a new song titled "**Where We Are**."
2. My neighbors' trampoline was so much fun that we jumped all day!
3. he
4. mouse
5. rarely
6. thinnest

Day 108
1. Answers will vary.
2. It is Frank's opinion that the best time to do your homework is after dinner.
3. farmer, tractor, field
4. spend
5. I, myself, I
6. amount

ANSWER KEY (cont.)

Day 109
1. "I love to play in the sprinklers on a hot day!" Ruby exclaimed.
2. the peanut butter jar's label
3. Aunt Maria made **her** famous chili for the barbecue.
4. Answers will vary.
5. Answers will vary.
6. mouth

Day 110
1. "I am not sure why people always take the shortcut to school," observed Jack.
2. The baby's bottle was empty, so he started to scream.
3. The zoo train **went** by the visitors, and everyone **heard** the whistle.
4. silently
5. adjective
6. cutest

Day 111
1. "I'd like to walk to the river and sit on the rocks," Nina said.
2. the tree's bark
3. are
4. the, reclining, the, living
5. Answers will vary.
6. hare

Day 112
1. Wes shouted, "I love going to school!"
2. the lion's tail
3. more tired
4. mouse
5. brightly, happily
6. early

Day 113
1. 6044 West Grant Blvd. San Francisco, CA 89004
2. Answers will vary.
3. but
4. Oliver **played** video games until dinnertime.
5. keep, scolded
6. choosing

Day 114
1. Aunt Vivian is traveling to Cairo, Egypt, this summer to see the pyramids.
2. Pablo's ears
3. sticky
4. Answers will vary.
5. Answers will vary.
6. morning

Day 115
1. "I wonder if there will be a goody bag at the birthday party," Jessica commented.
2. the teacher's computer
3. The mother cat **slept** in the sun while the kittens **played** around her.
4. rode
5. or
6. taking

Day 116
1. 603 Grainger Blvd. Alameda, CA 89004
2. the book's ending
3. but
4. The, rude, the, angry, the, frustrated
5. Sam and Jack **swam** in the pool to stay cool.
6. Answers will vary.

Day 117
1. I am going to ask my mom to buy me the album with the song titled "**Life Goes On**."
2. Lance's fishing pole
3. a, helpful
4. I **taught** my friend how to play soccer.
5. loudly
6. tripped

Day 118
1. "I wish you two would stop fighting over the video game!" Mom pleaded.
2. Teresa's teacher was absent on Friday.
3. louder
4. Answers will vary.
5. surprised
6. Answers will vary.

Day 119
1. Mr. Winters called out, "Who is buying lunch today?"
2. the soccer goalie's uniform
3. his, he
4. Answers will vary.
5. Answers will vary.
6. forget

Day 120
1. Answers will vary.
2. Miss Jones's bike
3. hungriest
4. Answers will vary.
5. Answers will vary.
6. spotted

ANSWER KEY *(cont.)*

Day 121
1. Answers will vary.
2. "How are we going to celebrate my birthday?" Jessie wondered.
3. warned
4. a, fluffy
5. Answers will vary.
6. fur

Day 122
1. "Who was the first person to finish the test?" Cal wondered.
2. Maria's saxophone
3. saddest
4. ox
5. loudly
6. curl

Day 123
1. I decided to read my poem titled "**Summer Fun**" for the poetry fair.
2. Answers will vary.
3. quiet, his
4. The artist **made** the painting in her art studio.
5. Answers will vary.
6. Answers will vary.

Day 124
1. I made up a dance to the song that is titled "**Jump, Jump, Jump**."
2. "Olive, can you come to my birthday party?" Kate asked.
3. her
4. Answers will vary.
5. The puppies **will cuddle** up to their mother.
6. touch

Day 125
1. The ballet class performed to the song "**Slow Symphony**."
2. The nurse said, "I am sorry, but I have to give you a shot."
3. given
4. happily
5. argued
6. our

Day 126
1. I have to write a book report on a book titled **In Mother's Memory**.
2. "I hope you have a really great birthday," Mom said to me this morning.
3. but
4. The, small, its
5. I **tore** the paper to make a collage for my art project.
6. Answers will vary.

Day 127
1. Our class published a book that is titled **Facts About Our Solar System**.
2. the dog's collar
3. we, our
4. I **woke** up first thing in the morning when the sun **came** up.
5. loudly
6. Answers will vary.

Day 128
1. 430 North Main Street Honolulu**,** HI 58998
2. The student's (or students') bullying was not tolerated at school.
3. The, blue, red
4. yet
5. were
6. Answers will vary.

Day 129
1. Kevin wanted to play *Football Mania* or *Truck-Race Warrior*.
2. the horse's saddle
3. most upset
4. Answers will vary.
5. were
6. circus

Day 130
1. Answers will vary.
2. "I really don't like having ants in my room!" shouted Leah.
3. Answers will vary.
4. Answers will vary.
5. Answers will vary.
6. stopped

Day 131
1. "I can't believe it is almost spring break!" Johnny exclaimed.
2. Henry's mom and Alana's dad were both chaperones on the field trip.
3. cry
4. Answers will vary.
5. wrote
6. careful

ANSWER KEY *(cont.)*

Day 132

1. I read the book **Sophie's Adventure** at the library.
2. a friend's game
3. he
4. Answers will vary.
5. red, brown
6. joyful

Day 133

1. "Should we go to the library or the park first?" Mom asked.
2. Jack's group is still getting its work done.
3. I, you
4. later
5. swim
6. quieter

Day 134

1. brand names
2. my friend's mother
3. Hank **wanted** to go to the lake and fish all day.
4. Answers will vary.
5. made
6. wrinkle

Day 135

1. titles
2. Gus wasn't sure that the pool's heater was turned on because the water's temperature was so low.
3. warmest
4. quickly
5. paid
6. darken

Day 136

1. I watched my friends play the video game titled *Public Arena*.
2. "Who should be on our team for kickball?" Lisa wondered.
3. Air pollution **was** a huge problem, and companies **were** part of the problem.
4. The, brown, the, icy, fresh
5. cars, drivers
6. major

Day 137

1. Answers will vary.
2. our school's cafeteria
3. sing
4. moose
5. quickly, safely
6. wonder

Day 138

1. Answers will vary.
2. The teacher's (or teachers') plan for the day was to get the students' desks cleaned out.
3. The teaching staff **decides** to honor the best students.
4. most famous
5. allowed
6. preview

Day 139

1. 276 West Road
   Concord, NH 29855
2. Avery's bird would not stop chirping, so Avery's mother had to cover the cage.
3. Scientists, whales, patterns
4. Answers will vary.
5. begins
6. poet

Day 140

1. Mexico City, Mexico, is a capital city that I would like to visit.
2. The dog park is closed because the park's gates are broken and the dogs' safety is at risk.
3. The bald eagle **will soar** over the blue river.
4. Answers will vary.
5. roamed
6. Answers will vary.

Day 141

1. Answers will vary.
2. Hannah's sweater is very special because her mother's sister made it for her.
3. will stop
4. Answers will vary.
5. caught
6. unlock

Day 142

1. The poem "**Party Time**" was written by a famous poet.
2. Answers will vary.
3. soon
4. Answers will vary.
5. The, funny, harmless, the
6. tough

Day 143

1. Answers will vary.
2. Answers will vary.
3. yummy, cheese, crisp
4. found
5. itself
6. happiness

ANSWER KEY (cont.)

Day 144
1. titles of books
2. Olivia's pencil
3. Sylvia **fed** her cat and **set** the table at night.
4. Answers will vary.
5. paid
6. hopeless

Day 145
1. 8920 Applegate Street Houston**,** TX 90221
2. The seal's whiskers were moving as he looked for food.
3. but
4. quickly
5. meant
6. hoped

Day 146
1. Ted wrote a poem and titled it "**Days Go On** and **On**."
2. the airplane's engine
3. softer
4. sheep
5. playfully, happily
6. Answers will vary.

Day 147
1. Every holiday, we sing the same silly song, "**Those Were** the **Days**."
2. Frank commented, **"I wonder what will be on our math test today."**
3. ate
4. The, beautiful, bright, red
5. Would the **men** be able to check my ticket before I enter?
6. instead

Day 148
1. "One of these days, I want to learn how to play guitar," Donny said.
2. "I hope that Paul's toy is not broken because of Jake's mistake," John commented.
3. quickly
4. Finn's dad was a great soccer coach, and all the players respected **him**.
5. the, rainiest
6. breakfast

Day 149
1. song titles
2. the house's roof
3. run
4. Answers will vary.
5. I, my
6. careful

Day 150
1. The audience wanted to hear the song titled "**Tender Kisses**" at the concert.
2. Kevin's aunt and uncle are the nicest people in the world.
3. Maya's mom was going to drive **herself** to work.
4. cheerfully
5. The, small, faster, the, big
6. sweater

Day 151
1. 759 Walnut Blvd. Tampa Bay**,** FL 58990
2. "Who do you think would have taken my bike?" Patrick wondered.
3. librarian, Drew, book
4. Answers will vary.
5. wrote
6. flood

Day 152
1. "Mom, will you sing '**Hello My Baby**' to me like you used to?" Ella asked.
2. Hal's music teacher wished that Hal's practice time would increase.
3. her
4. Answers will vary.
5. new
6. Answers will vary.

Day 153
1. 5894 Harvard Place New Haven**,** UT 84770
2. The principal's secretary was in charge of calling parents.
3. hard
4. she
5. wait
6. Answers will vary.

Day 154
1. Noah's robot
2. the mad scientist's time machine
3. Answers will vary.
4. and
5. stung
6. believe

ANSWER KEY *(cont.)*

Day 155

1. "Mom, when will I be able to walk to school by myself?" Oscar wondered.
2. Carter's baseball team was able to beat Luke's baseball team.
3. boat, shore, dock
4. quickly
5. pride
6. neither

Day 156

1. Grandpa always sings "**Long, Long Ago**" to his grandchildren.
2. Answers will vary.
3. his
4. The, brave, the, cold, ocean
5. teeth
6. clothes

Day 157

1. If you translate the song title from Spanish, it is called "**Oh, Promise Me**."
2. the princess's gown
3. our
4. child
5. playfully
6. moist

Day 158

1. Answers will vary.
2. We went to my grandma's house for a barbecue.
3. him
4. traveled
5. class, costumes, play
6. Answers will vary.

Day 159

1. Dad asked, "Are we going to have time to go to the track meet?"
2. Fiona's scarf
3. Answers will vary.
4. Answers will vary.
5. having
6. royal

Day 160

1. I would like to publish my poem titled "**Rainy Days**" in our class poetry book.
2. The neighbor's house is very scary, so Tanner's mom helped us get our ball back.
3. their
4. Answers will vary.
5. Answers will vary.
6. Answers will vary.

Day 161

1. Answers will vary.
2. the baby's bottle
3. adjective
4. Answers will vary.
5. found
6. mouth

Day 162

1. Wade announced, "The theater is finally showing the movie *Truck Race*!"
2. Christina's new jeans
3. Answers will vary.
4. Answers will vary.
5. The, bright
6. preschool

Day 163

1. Answers will vary.
2. Ava asked, "Can I have a little more time to work on my assignment?"
3. its
4. Answers will vary.
5. is
6. uncover

Day 164

1. Answers will vary.
2. the fire's spark
3. Answers will vary.
4. Answers will vary.
5. got
6. Answers will vary.

Day 165

1. Answers will vary.
2. Mom commented, "I thought your friends were all polite at your party."
3. were
4. continually
5. heard
6. Answers will vary.

Day 166

1. Carla remembers her dad singing a song titled "**School Days**" to her.
2. "Do you think I should go to the party?" Marty wondered.
3. her
4. Answers will vary.
5. see
6. Answers will vary.

ANSWER KEY *(cont.)*

Day 167
1. Answers will vary.
2. Lucas's toothbrush
3. Answers will vary.
4. Answers will vary.
5. stayed
6. Answers will vary.

Day 168
1. Answers will vary.
2. "What is on the menu for school lunch today?" Nick wondered.
3. Answers will vary.
4. wanted
5. we, ourselves
6. island

Day 169
1. Answers will vary.
2. the airplane's wing
3. lion, meal
4. Answers will vary.
5. see
6. Answers will vary.

Day 170
1. I used to love the song "**This Old Man**" when I was little.
2. Jimmy's pet snake and Ken's pet hamster should never be left in the same cage!
3. left
4. Answers will vary.
5. Answers will vary.
6. settle

Day 171
1. Answers will vary.
2. "Mr. Scott, I really wish you would be my teacher again next year," Ezra said.
3. Answers will vary.
4. Answers will vary.
5. lost
6. Answers will vary.

Day 172
1. Ben likes to talk to other kids online about the video game *Power Works*.
2. my dad's car
3. his
4. looked, touched
5. gently
6. leader

Day 173
1. Answers will vary.
2. decide
3. The, bright
4. helped
5. sat
6. babies

Day 174
1. Answers will vary.
2. Answers will vary.
3. sat, worked, felt
4. Answers will vary.
5. began
6. limb

Day 175
1. Answers will vary.
2. Answers will vary.
3. was
4. precisely
5. drove
6. Answers will vary.

Day 176
1. Answers will vary.
2. my neighbor's house
3. Martin and Will **hiked** up to the waterfall, and they **saw** a lot of wildlife.
4. red, blue, the
5. generously
6. Answers will vary.

Day 177
1. 49300 West Kingston Road Newport Beach, CA 98800
2. Answers will vary.
3. Adventurous, the, slimy, wet
4. man
5. endlessly
6. Answers will vary.

Day 178
1. Answers will vary.
2. the animal's body part
3. her
4. third graders, cafeteria
5. proud
6. Answers will vary.

Day 179
1. movie titles
2. Michael's baseball
3. a, comfortable, green
4. Answers will vary.
5. see
6. Answers will vary.

Day 180
1. "I hope our choir does not have to learn "**This Train's A-Coming**" because it's a silly song," Greta complained.
2. Lance's handbook tells the scouts that their troop's destination is miles away.
3. Answers will vary.
4. gracefully
5. was
6. Answers will vary.

REFERENCES CITED

Haussamen, Brock. 2014. "Some Questions and Answers About Grammar." Retrieved from http://www.ateg.org/grammar/qna.php.

Hillocks, George, Jr., and Michael W. Smith. 1991. "Grammar and Usage." In *Handbook of Research on Teaching the English Language Arts*. James Flood, Julie M. Jensen, Diane Lapp, and James R. Squire. New York: Macmillan.

Hodges, Richard E. 1991. "The Conventions of Writing." In *Handbook of Research on Teaching the English Language Arts*. James Flood, Julie M. Jensen, Diane Lapp, and James R. Squire. New York: Macmillan.

———. 2003. "Grammar and Literacy Learning." In *Handbook of Research on Teaching the English Language Arts*, 2nd ed. James Flood, Julie M. Jensen, Diane Lapp, and James R. Squire. New York: Macmillan.

Lederer, Richard. 1987. *Anguished English: An Anthology of Accidental Assaults upon Our Language.* New York: Dell.

Marzano, Robert J. 2010. When Practice Makes Perfect. . .Sense. *Educational Leadership* 68(3): 81–83.

Truss, Lynne. 2003. *Eats, Shoots and Leaves: The Zero Tolerance Approach to Punctuation.* New York: Gotham Books.

CONTENTS OF THE DIGITAL RESOURCE CD

Teacher Resources

Resource	Filename
Diagnostic Assessment Directions	directions.pdf
Practice Page Item Analysis	pageitem.pdf
	pageitem.doc
	pageitem.xls
Student Item Analysis	studentitem.pdf
	studentitem.doc
	studentitem.xls
Standards Chart	standards.pdf

Student Resources

All of the 180 practice pages are contained in a single PDF. In order to print specific days, open the PDF and select the pages to print.

Resource	Filename
Practice Pages Day 1–Day 180	practicepages.pdf